WHITE ANXIETY

WHITE ANXIETY

HOW CONSERVATIVES CONVINCE AMERICA'S VOTERS TO ACT AGAINST THEIR ECONOMIC INTERESTS

DOUGLAS HINES

HINES PRESS

Hines Press

Decatur, Georgia

1. American Politics
2. Party Politics
3. American Economics
4. American History
5. African American History

Paperback ISBN: 979-8-9949415-9-1

Hardcover ISBN: 979-8-9949415-2-2

Ebook ISBN: 979-8-9949415-5-3

Audiobook ISBN: 979-8-9949415-8-4

Library of Congress Control Number 2026910731

Editorial Production by Lantern Literary, LLC

Front Cover Design by Emily's World of Design

In memory of my mom and dad:
Dad always said, when he was around my age, that he wanted to use his knowledge to help people.
Dad challenged me to do the same. I bring his knowledge and wisdom with me.
That said, my dad would not have known as much as he knew, accomplished as much as he did, or had such a big smile on his face all the time without the brilliance of my mom. Her wisdom and encouragement sustain me.

CONTENTS

Preface ix
Introduction xvii

1. We Need Two Productive Parties 1
2. What Are Conservatives? 23
3. What Are Liberals? 45
4. How White Anxiety Works 57
5. Let's Think with Our Heads 77
6. How White Anxiety Thrives 99
7. Conservatives and White Anxiety's History 109
8. Republicans and Bad Economies 129
9. Poor Performance and Bad Behavior 139
10. Conservatives Must Come Clean 149
11. Wealth Concentration Hurts Us All 157
12. Democrats Must Message 167
13. Steps Toward Better Choices 179
14. Conclusion 189

Notes 193
Index 197
About the Author 201

PREFACE

After the last presidential election, I began to think that no one saw what I did—that what was obvious to me might not be so to everyone else. Before I expand on that, it is worth noting that I am typically not the type of person who thinks I have special revelations about the world. I believe that there is nothing new under the sun.

As a software engineer, I excel at math, logic, probability, and statistics. I excel at recognizing patterns because my mind works overtime to uncover how the seemingly disparate pieces of a subject fit together. When they do not initially fit, my mind never stops trying different permutations of how to position those pieces, involuntarily searching for explanations. Our choice for president in 2024 did not fit.

I thought to myself, that November, "I have spent decades of my life watching the country make bad decisions about who to elect as president, and I can't make it make sense...." But people do not just make seemingly ignorant decisions en masse without some underlying explanation. Most Americans can spot good and bad people. They can even spot trends. But for some reason, many of the candidates Republicans helped to elect, the ones whose reputations and track records should have raised red flags, slipped right past smart American voters.

And perhaps others *did* see it. But no books or programs talk about that pattern. I know enough history and have lived long enough to not only see the pattern but express what I see in a way that most people will understand.

My dad spotted the trend a long time ago.

We called my father's business "The Shop." He and his brothers opened their auto repair shop in the 1950s. They had moved to Detroit from North Carolina during the Great Migration. They worked together in their business. Collision repair was my father's part of the business. His brothers worked on engines, transmissions, front-end alignments, and every other aspect of auto repair. That shop proved key to my understanding of the economy.

The shop bustled with activity. Finished cars left with a new shine, while new wrecks arrived all mangled and on the backs of wreckers. A Ford parts truck might swoop in, double-park, and make a delivery. The paint store would send over boxes filled with masking tape, cans of paint, stirrers, and funnels. We would hear the constant hum of sanders on body panels, preparing cars for the paint booth. It was a magical place.

I grew up going "down the shop," as we would say, in elementary school. On Saturdays, my father allowed one or more of his twelve sons to go with him to work. In our younger years, we made money by making trips to the corner store for the workers or the retirees who sat under a massive shade tree out in front of the shop. They let us kids keep some of the change. We also swept the work areas of the shop for money.

I started performing actual work on cars in the eighth grade, shortly after I turned thirteen, starting with an orange Chevy Vega with a small dent on the hood. I was ecstatic and beaming with pride. I had only fixed dents on old toolboxes up until that point.

In the ten years that I worked for my father, he solved problems I thought were unsolvable. After working all day without success on a problem, I would call him over. Within minutes, my father would have the solution. He was the first genius I had ever met.

When I was an older teen riding to work in my father's wrecker, he told me that Republican presidents mess up the economy when they take office. He did not explain why or how. He gave me no evidence.

But that simple statement from my hero, mentor, genius dad stuck with me. I trusted my father's judgment. His assessment of Republican presidents lingered in my mind, though I had no information to prove or disprove it.

The proof showed up in our personal and professional lives. During elementary and junior high school, we experienced twenty-seven months of the recessions that occurred during Richard Nixon's presidency. My father's business and our household suffered as a result.

By the 1980 presidential election, I had reached voting age. After arriving home from Morehouse College during the spring of 1982, I went to work for my dad. While I was home, he introduced me to a beautiful young teacher who would later become my wife. We married in the middle of the Ronald Reagan's 1983 recession.

As a married couple, my wife and I started filing our taxes jointly. She had inherited her mother's property in Detroit before I met her, and that property became part of our federal tax filing. The federal tax policy passed by Reagan began to affect us directly. We saw tax increases tied to that property, and the 1984 FICA deductions topped the 1983 FICA deductions.

I was beginning to learn a hard lesson. I had started college under Jimmy Carter, but I was working under Reagan—two different economic situations. I was reminded of my father's wisdom.

In 1984, we welcomed our first child into the world during the Reagan recession. The economy had suffered widespread job losses. Thankfully, we had moved to the southwestern part of the country right after we married. My wife and I both had good jobs at a university. We had health insurance. We lived in oil country. So, the recession did not seem as bad as it could have.

At that point, I was not deeply engaged in politics. But I did listen to the Iran–Contra hearings during Reagan's second term. I had just started a software business with a partner, so I worked from home. The hearings played in my house five days a week on C-SPAN.

I also listened to local news and talk radio. Eventually, I began listening to Rush Limbaugh, partly out of curiosity. He offered a clear window into how Conservatives thought—something that was not easy to access at the time.

As I listened and the internet began to take shape, I paid closer attention.

That's when something shifted for me. I would experience events one way, and then I would listen to Rush and learn that Conservatives had a completely different understanding and different feelings about the same events. At first, that surprised me. Their take on politics and how the country should work baffled me. I knew what I felt and understood. However, they tried to convince me that what I felt was not real.

They explained how my feelings were guided by the liberal media. I felt insulted. I knew my taxes went up. That was a fact. But they tried to convince me that Reagan cut taxes. I knew the economy went into recession under Carter and Reagan. They tried to convince me that Conservatives produced much better economies. They also directly contradicted the smartest mentor in my life, my father.

Reagan had raised FICA taxes from 5.5 percent to 7.65 percent, phased in over seven years. FICA taxes have no exemptions or deductions. The rate began to increase immediately. So with each increase, the government pulled more money from our paychecks. At the same time, the national debt rose faster than it ever had. Yet Rush praised Reagan's fiscal policy.

After Reagan's years were over, George H. W. Bush (Bush Sr.) took office. During Bush Sr.'s recession, Rush acted as if we had imagined the whole recession. He acted as if the recession was a news media creation. But it felt the same as the previous ones to me. The auto industry was hit hard again. Though I no longer lived in Detroit, and I could not go back and help my father anymore, I knew his business suffered with it.

Bush's administration caused me to pay much more attention. I listened to Rush and the news every day. I also got more involved in church, learning more about the Gospel and teaching Bible classes. I began to understand much better what my father told me about life and about the Bible. My research became more intentional as the internet developed. I could personally experience a political event and then see the same event through the eyes of people around the world in AOL chat rooms, which were among the first online communities on the internet.

Over time, one thing became clear.

There was a growing dissonance between current events and the way Conservatives described them. What I saw with my own eyes was not what Conservatives were reporting. I experienced one thing, but Rush told me I saw something else. Eventually, I had to make a decision: trust my own judgment or adopt theirs.

Finally, I decided to challenge this pattern directly. I called Rush's radio program year after year, but I never got through. Then I noticed nearly all the callers he took agreed with his perspective on the economy and politics. They just said, "Ditto" at the beginning of their commentary. He rarely took calls from callers with opposing points of view—and when he did, the callers seemed unprepared.

It got more frustrating. Then frustration became resolve. The more I learned, the more I realized that, as chaotic as the economy had gotten, no one was coming to save us.

I've seen the same pattern repeatedly since Reagan and George H. W. Bush. I decided to write this book because I finally discovered why it happens. I have gathered enough information and gained enough confidence to know that what I have witnessed is real. The famous Malian writer and historian Amadou Hampâté Bâ once said, "Every time an old man dies, it is as if a library has burned down." I have lived more years than I'm going to live. I decided to publish part of my library before the whole thing burns to the ground.

I can tie nearly every major economic downturn or disaster in our country during my lifetime to the economics of Conservatives. Apart from Carter's recession, every economic recession during my life, even to this day, began during a Republican presidential administration.

In fact, Republican administrations hold all the worst economic records. Republicans have presided over economies that have set records in everything from foreclosures to bank failures to bankruptcies to the piling up of our national debt. Conservatives' economic policies have put them at the top of the heap of economic downturn and disaster in America since Herbert Hoover in 1929.

After Republican presidents and their economic policies cause those disasters, Republican candidates lose elections. However, after the smoke clears and the economy stabilizes, they come right back, selling their same economic snake oil. When times are good, for some reason, that snake oil sells well again.

Wait a minute now! What about the Liberals? What about the Democrats? I'm sure they have economic disasters!

What if they do not? What if Democratic economies and Republican economies look completely different? Should I make some fantastical statement just to keep things evenhanded? Should I tie myself into rhetorical knots just to seem fair? Should I just make something up so some aren't annoyed by this seeming hit piece? I can be politically correct or tell the truth. I cannot do both. I choose to tell the truth.

Electing a Republican as president makes our economy quite vulnerable. Based on America's history since the Great Depression, we statistically have nearly a 100 percent chance of suffering a recession if we elect a Republican president.[i] Every time we have elected a Republican President, the economy experienced a recession during their administration. The numbers during that time period break down like this:

- Recessions occurred during 100 percent of Republican presidential administrations.
- Recessions occurred during 75 percent of Republican presidents' second terms.
- The annual federal budget deficit increased during 100 percent of Republican presidential administrations by the time they left office.
- Every Republican presidential administration left office with unemployment rates at or over 5.5 percent.[ii]

Some might think I made those numbers up. The numbers are real. And numbers do not lie. Check the references from BLS and NBER. No one can predict the future with 100 percent certainty. However, we can look at past performance as a window to the future. Predictions based on performance will likely give us a reliable picture of the future.

And those who keep supporting the economics of Conservatives, as bad as probability tells us that outcome will be, just give Conservatives license to keep making our prospects worse.

Imagine a business that gave poor service to its customers, but in spite of that poor service, those same customers still patronized it. And no matter how many corners the business cut or how badly it treated its customers, customers continued to patronize it. As long as the business kept growing, the business owner might see no need to improve customer service. In fact, the customer service might continue to get worse.

That's the situation with the economics of Conservatives and their governance today. This lack of accountability comes from the license White Anxiety gives Conservatives to do whatever they want without consequence until the economy goes into recession. White Anxiety is a fear tactic that induces anxiety in the minds of White voters against "others." Conservative candidates use White Anxiety to manipulate the hearts and minds of voters.

So, I cannot balance "both sides." Liberals have nothing that rivals the long history and depth of White Anxiety. Nor do modern Democratic administrations have comparable economic numbers. This phenomenon is unique to Conservatives. Modern Democrats and modern Republicans are not equally culpable for White Anxiety, any more than they produce equal economies.

Martin Luther King said about Americans that we are in an "inescapable network of mutuality, tied in a single garment of destiny." King also said in that letter: "Whatever affects one directly affects all indirectly."[iii] We cannot continue to rip that garment into shreds, partially sew it back together, then rip it up again. When we do, we only hurt ourselves.

Perhaps discussing White Anxiety will help victims recognize it. Hopefully, those voters will also help others to avoid falling victim to it as political actors attempt to spread it. Perhaps all of us will recognize the power we have to determine who represents us—and we will use that power to stop falling victim to these mind tricks.

INTRODUCTION

People don't always remember what we have done for them—but they certainly remember how we made them feel. In the fifth grade, I had a teacher named Mrs. Taylor. She was, at the time, not the nicest person to me. She did not smile much. She did not compliment a lot. But what she did was magic. She made each student feel like we could do anything if we worked hard enough. She held us to a standard and never let up. I cannot think of a single academic thing she taught me, but it has been over fifty years, and I still remember how she made me feel. Maya Angelou expressed that sentiment on many occasions.

Our feelings are powerful. They motivate us to do many things, good and bad. Research shows that negative feelings cause the strongest reactions.[i] When we feel like someone has or will hurt us, we react quite powerfully. I'm not sure why our brains function that way, but they do. Perhaps it's a survival mechanism.

In America, throughout our history, politicians have exploited White voters through their feelings about others. Politicians have fed them negative perceptions of non-Whites and immigrants. Those same politicians manipulated voters, guiding them to support Conservatives no matter what. They also groomed voters to avoid their perceived enemies, the Liberals.

America emerged on the world stage as a multi-class system. Most societies follow that pattern based on wealth and heredity. America's initial classes were not only based on wealth and privilege, though. America also based its class system on skin color. America assigned more value to white skin than to black skin. That determination was carried out in law at all levels of government, from the local level to the Supreme Court.

Even after America amended its constitution and laws, parts of the country maintained the class system through domestic terrorism. Local law enforcement supported that terrorism. Organizations like the Ku Klux Klan and White Citizens' Councils—and legal frameworks such as Black Codes—enforced the continuation of that race-based class system through violence and a heavy-handed legal apparatus.

Eventually, the Supreme Court struck down support for that class system at the federal level. Federal law superseded state and local laws and customs that supported the old class system, forcing the entire nation to respect all races equally. Laws could no longer prop up class systems like racial segregation or ballot box restrictions through trickery and violence.

Sounds good, doesn't it? America had a skin-color-based class system enforced by state and local law—and we fixed it.

Not so fast. We fixed it *on paper*. Unfortunately, governments cannot legislate morality.

And in this specific case, there's a natural geographic dividing line between the states that fought to preserve that race-based system and those that didn't. We find that line at 36°30' north latitude. That's the line drawn during the Missouri Compromise of 1820, separating the slave-labor states from the free-labor states and territories at the time.[ii] Today, we call the two sides of that line the North and the South.

In fact, the states that fought in the Civil War to maintain a race-based economic system have become the political base for Conservatives. Conservative politicians work hard to exploit those voters even today. The parents, grandparents, and great-grandparents of White voters, in many cases, held on to the traditions of those who attempted to start their own country to preserve the American chattel slavery system when they felt it was close to collapse.

I imagine that the Republican Party reaps the benefit of voters' preference for Conservatives. After all, politicians use whatever advantage they can to get elected. Democrats do that too. But even if our preferences are being influenced, when we compare politicians under the microscope and decide we prefer one politician over another, we are making a choice. If we look at a specific candidate's record and decide that candidate deserves election or reelection, we cast our vote with confidence.

But what if a candidate entered a voter's house on Election Day and slipped a drug into their coffee that altered their mood, causing them to vote for that candidate and no other?

I want to talk about White Anxiety as exactly that kind of drug. In this hypothetical scenario, the voter did not vote for the candidate based on anything the candidate did or did not do. The voter chose the candidate because of the drug. White Anxiety creates a condition of persistent fear for the future in the minds of White voters. It makes them fear non-Whites and immigrants as threats to their way of life.

This book will help us to understand how Conservatives have used —and continue to use—the feelings of White Americans to plant in their minds the idea that they must always vote for Conservatives, never for Liberals. Both feelings must flourish in the minds of White voters to accomplish their exploitation. Conservatives need the drug to take effect on Election Day, every Election Day.

If Republicans convince voters to vote based on their feelings rather than policy, competence, economic interest, or judgment, Conservatives can sell them any candidate, no matter how flawed. Republicans can sell those under the influence of White Anxiety any set of policies, even if those policies will hurt them directly. They can even sell them on political violence. But this only works if Republicans convince White voters that Republicans' policies will keep their competition at bay.

During his 2016 campaign, Donald Trump exposed the long-term effects of that exploitation. At a campaign rally in Iowa, Trump said to a cheering crowd, "I could stand in the middle of Fifth Avenue and shoot somebody, and I wouldn't lose any voters."[iii] Trump was comfortable making that statement because he knew the exploited White electorate felt they had no choice but to vote for him. Republicans had succeeded at White Anxiety. Several major negative revelations surfaced about Trump throughout that election cycle. He still won.

If Conservatives had a record of great policy results, they would win on those results. They do not. Conservatives hold records for the following:

- Leaving office with the highest federal budget deficits[iv]
- Increasing the national debt by the largest percentage during a presidential administration
- Spawning the greatest number of recessions[v]
- Spawning the worst recessions, including the Great Depression
- Spawning the longest recessions
- Leaving office with the highest unemployment numbers[vi]

In fact, if Republicans ran on what they actually do in office, they might never win another presidential election.

Some might ask: What about everything else Republicans have accomplished? They may have an economic track record of recessions, high unemployment, and high deficits, but what about the things they do right?

The economy is my focus in this book. My morality springs from my religion, Christianity. I study it. I live it. I teach it. I lead by it. I do not want or need the government to get involved in that part of my life. I would hope that members of the government lived by my religion. Individuals, in government and out, must make those decisions for themselves. However, I want the government to manage the economy such that, if I work hard and manage my affairs well, I can make a decent living and provide for my family.

But White Anxiety is not a governing strategy. It's a strategy Conservatives use to attain or maintain power. It's horrible for governing a country, and the White people who vote for Republicans are, in some cases, just as negatively affected as everyone else. Conservatives never plan to improve the lives of White Anxiety's victims. They want to gain power and carry out the ultimate goals of conservatism: reduce the effectiveness of the federal government and enrich their friends. They want to emasculate the federal government so that it does not limit them or their donors in any way, shape, or form in their efforts to concentrate wealth.

In this book, I'll discuss our country's need for two competent governing parties—what makes the Republican Party ineffective based on its economic history, and what makes them so effective at getting elected despite that record.

I'll examine what makes a person a Conservative in America. That may sound easy, but the word "Conservative" is an identity label, and defining an identity label like "Conservative" presents the same challenge as defining "mauve" as an identity label. We can describe mauve, the color. But what do we mean when we call something or someone "a mauve?" Most of us misunderstand what the label "a Conservative" means in American politics and governance. I'll use history and practice to clarify it.

People who call themselves Conservatives sometimes do so in error. They may hold one or two moral positions that feel conservative, but as many will discover, that doesn't make them Conservatives in the political sense.

Next, I will discuss what makes a person a Liberal in America. More than ever, our country chooses its representatives from two parties: Democrats and Republicans. Republicans are the Conservatives, and Democrats are the Liberals. I will examine why, based on history. I will show how Conservatives in former Confederate states used White Anxiety to deny Black citizens their right to vote. I will also chronicle the journey of the former Confederate states from the Democratic Party to the Republican Party in the 1960s.

I will talk about White Anxiety, how it works, and the economic problems caused by selecting Republican candidates for president or to Congress. The lack of accountability—a major side effect of anxiety-based politics—does great damage to the country and to the Republican Party.

I will review economic information that makes the case for reforming our government. We must better understand what we want to do, both as the American people and as individuals.

Finally, I will explore ways to make our country better by getting beyond the grip of emotion-driven voting. I will talk about how to identify candidates who want to heighten our emotions and find ways to arm ourselves with information rather than allowing candidates and news outlets to groom us.

We must each answer this question for ourselves: "What can we as the American people accomplish through the actions of the federal government?"

Our answers might surprise us. We might discover we align more with Liberals than Conservatives—or we might find that those who call themselves Conservatives have done so correctly. Either way, we must each make that informed decision on our own, without fear, pressure, or anxiety. We cannot make serious voting decisions based on feelings.

Key to our decision-making process is performance information about the top of each of those two parties. We hear constantly that America should be a meritocracy. Fine. Let's hold both parties to that standard and look at how each one performs when it comes to economic issues. That will tell us who merits our vote—and who does not.

CHAPTER 1
WE NEED TWO PRODUCTIVE PARTIES

> *We need presidents who understand the importance of the economy, not just to our comfort, but to our survival as a country. For a government to be effective, it must concern itself with bringing about and sustaining a growing economy."*

KEEP THE ECONOMY GROWING

WHEN WARREN BUFFETT invested in a company, he took it on as part of his enterprise, Berkshire Hathaway, and left a CEO in charge. Buffett had two rules for those CEOs:

Rule #1: Never lose money.[i]

Rule #2: Never forget rule #1.

Buffett made his CEOs live by those rules. Money is the lifeblood of any company. Drain it, and the company dies. Simple as that.

Governments are not companies. As much as some people want them to operate like companies, they cannot. But those who run our government also run our economy. They should live by a similar set of rules:

Rule #1: Keep the economy growing.
Rule #2: Never forget rule #1.

The survival of our country depends on a growing economy. Rule #1 isn't a preference. It is a necessity.

When candidates seek elective office in America, they will most likely do so through either the Democratic or Republican Party. These are both old and experienced parties with long histories, but they differ greatly in how they govern and manage the economy. The way each party handles the economy should matter greatly to every American citizen because they each produce wildly different results.

Though some voters argue about differences in any given administration's policy, they cannot argue the success or failure of the economy run under that administration. We determine economic success or failure using numbers. Our government reports on its own economic results every month. The numbers speak for themselves.

I studied math in high school and college. I took as much math as they offered in high school. Math always felt comfortable to me. Unlike writing or historical interpretation, math is objective. I argued with my English professor about how she marked my essays. I could never argue with my calculus teacher. No matter what that professor thought of me, she had to mark my solution to a math problem right or wrong based on the mathematical rules she taught me. Similarly, our evaluation of economic success relies on the same objective measures we see in mathematics.

We judge an administration's economic success or failure using simple math. When the economy grows, it produces more goods and services, and thereby higher gross domestic product (GDP) numbers. A growing economy requires more workers. So, growing economies employ more people and thereby reduce unemployment. Growing economies spell success for presidential administrations.

When an economy shrinks, the opposite happens. The economy produces fewer goods and services, thereby resulting in a lower GDP. A shrinking economy requires fewer workers, thereby increasing unemployment. Economists call those periods of economic downturn "recessions." Shrinking economies—recessions—demonstrate failure for presidential administrations.

TWO PARTIES, TWO ECONOMIC PHILOSOPHIES

Much of the difference in economic performance between Democrats and Republicans stems from their different philosophies. Democrats focus on the demand side of the economy—the workers, the people. Republicans focus on the supply side of the economy—the companies, the investors.

Supply-side economics is a modern economic theory. When our economy needs a boost, supply-side economic theory would have government funnel economic stimulus through corporations and investors. I assumed that, at some point in my study, I would understand the effectiveness of this economic theory. I have yet to see it work—not once, at the state or federal level. George H. W. Bush famously called supply-side economics "voodoo economics" during the 1980 Republican primaries.[ii] Bush went on to serve as Ronald Reagan's vice president, then as a one-term president. When Bush attempted to reverse some of Reagan's tax cut policy, the Republican Party primaried him during his reelection campaign. He lost the election to Bill Clinton and became the poster child for what happens to Republican presidents when they buck the system and try to move away from supply-side economics.

Since our economy depends greatly on consumer spending, the lower the number of people employed, the less the economy grows. It's a downward spiral. Supply-side economics would have us believe that companies and their investors drive the economy. When the economy needs a boost, supply-side practitioners believe that tax cuts for investors and companies will help the economy grow.

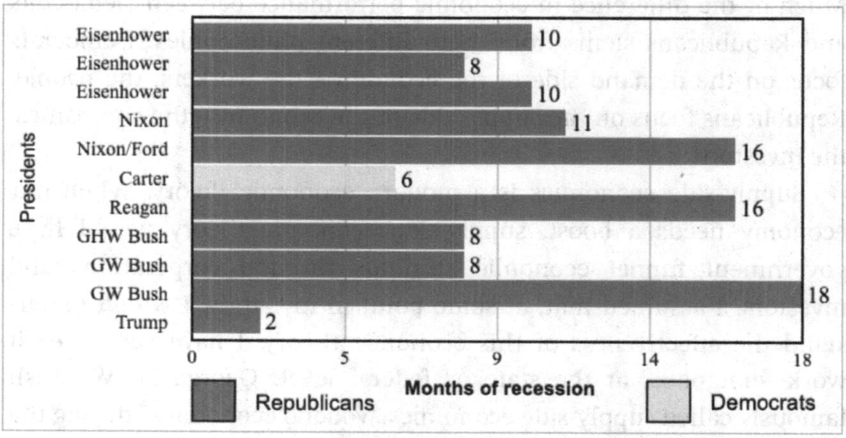

Figure 1: Recessions since 1953 (*National Bureau of Economic Research*)

Democrats follow the more traditional economic theory championed by the economist John Maynard Keynes. Keynesian economics focuses on the demand side of the economy, on consumer spending and job creation through increased demand for goods and services rather than the profit margins of companies and investors.[iii]

The results of these two philosophies show up clearly in whether—and how fast—the economy grows or contracts after each is applied.

Figure 1, from the National Bureau of Economic Research, shows shrinking economies—recessions—since 1953. Dwight D. Eisenhower took office in 1953 as the first Republican president elected since the Great Depression.[iv] That marked the beginning of the modern Republican era.

Each bar represents a separate recession; its length represents the recession's duration. Multiple bars for the same president mean his administration spawned multiple recessions. The chart contains seven presidents. Six are Republicans. One is a Democrat. Since 1953, Americans have elected six Republican presidents and six Democratic presidents. During the tenures of five of the six Democratic presidents, the economy experienced no recession, only growth.

Figure 1 shows that every Republican administration experienced at least one recession. Every two-term Republican administration, except Ronald Reagan's, experienced two or more recessions. Three of the six Republican presidents experienced recessions that lasted more than a year. Democrats succeed at growing the economy; Republicans fail.

The longest recession belongs to George W. Bush. That recession lasted a year and a half and threatened the economy so much and for so long that economists named it the Great Recession.

Figure 1 tells us three things:

- Every modern Republican administration produced a recession
- Republican recessions last an average of ten months
- The last Democratic recession happened under Jimmy Carter

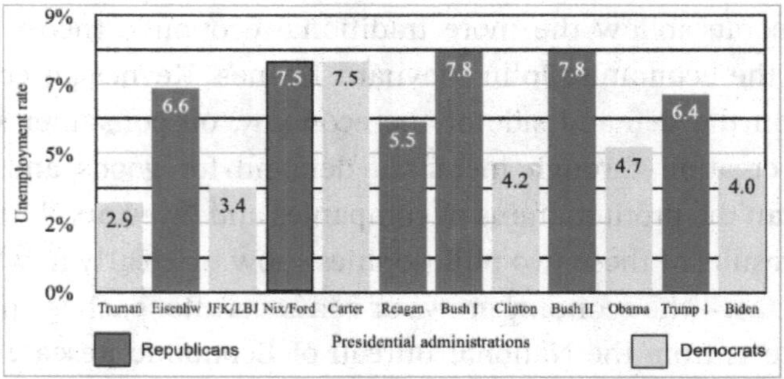

Figure 2: Ending unemployment rates since 1953 (*The Bureau of Labor Statistics - bls.gov*)

When the economy grows, people have jobs, unemployment falls, tax revenue rises, and the dollar strengthens. Savings increase. Investment increases. People buy homes.

When the economy shrinks, everything reverses. Jobs disappear. Young people entering adulthood or finishing college can't find work. Their plans, independence, families, and careers get pushed back or abandoned altogether.

The unemployment rate is another sign of the difference between the two economic philosophies.

Figure 2 shows unemployment rates at the end of each president's term since 1953. Shrinking economies produce higher unemployment rates. Growing economies produce lower unemployment rates.[v]

Along the bottom of Figure 2, we see each presidential administration since 1953. The vertical bars represent the unemployment rate when each administration left office. The taller bars represent higher unemployment. The shorter bars represent lower unemployment.

From Figure 2, we can conclude the following:

- Every Republican president left office with unemployment above 5 percent.
- Every Democratic president, except Carter, left office with unemployment below 5 percent.

If you compare figures 1 and 2, you'll also note that high unemployment correlates with recessions during this time period.

Growing economies produce low unemployment. Shrinking economies produce high unemployment. The party that grows the economy is effective. The party that shrinks it is not.

In Figure 2, when Harry Truman, a Democrat, left office in 1953, the unemployment rate was 2.9 percent. Dwight Eisenhower, a Republican, took office and served two terms. By the end of his second term, unemployment had risen to 6.6 percent. During Eisenhower's administration, America's economy experienced three recessions.

In 1960, John F. Kennedy, a Democrat, won the presidential election. Due to his assassination, Kennedy did not serve a full term. Lyndon Johnson took over Kennedy's presidency in 1963, while in the process of campaigning for the 1964 election. Johnson won the 1964 election and served a single term. By the time Johnson left office, unemployment had dropped to 3.4 percent.

In 1968, Richard Nixon, a Republican, won the election. Nixon served a full term and won reelection, but he resigned because of the Watergate scandal. Ford took over the presidency in 1974. Ford served the rest of Nixon's second term. By the time Ford left office, unemployment had risen to 7.5 percent.

The pattern is consistent. Democrats lower unemployment. Republicans raise it.

AMERICA'S SURVIVAL DEPENDS ON ITS ECONOMY

We cannot treat a growing economy as a "nice-to-have." We require it to sustain our country.

When Franklin D. Roosevelt took office, he inherited an economy already in the midst of a depression. Herbert Hoover, a Republican, had left an unemployment rate of 25 percent. When Roosevelt entered office, as he worked to pass the first part of his New Deal legislation, he knew the country's survival depended on the success of his policies.

When Roosevelt began to do his work, supposedly one of his friends said to him, "If the New Deal is a success, you will be remembered as the greatest president in American history. If it fails, you will be the worst one." In the story, Roosevelt replied, "If I fail, I will be remembered as the last one."

Roosevelt realized that our form of government would not continue if a large portion of our country's citizens could not make a living. It seems unthinkable, but even today, our country could devolve into the same chaos Roosevelt feared. During the Great Depression, many Americans lost their homes and could not afford food. We need presidents who understand the importance of the economy, not just to our comfort, but to our survival as a country. For a government to be effective, it must concern itself with bringing about and sustaining a growing economy.

In 2026, we must rely on one effective governing party. The Democratic Party creates and sustains growing economies. The Republican Party does not. That's just an economic reality. The economic statistics bear that out:

- A Republican administration presided over the worst economic depression in American history, the Great Depression. It began in 1929, during Herbert Hoover's only term as president.
- A Republican administration presided over the worst economic recession since the Great Depression. The Great Recession started in late 2007 during George W. Bush's second term. It remains the longest recession since the Great Depression.
- Every Republican administration since Hoover's has spawned a recession. During the seven Republican administrations since the Great Depression, we have seen ten recessions (figure 1).
- Every Republican administration since the Great Depression has left office with a larger budget deficit than when they entered office. The larger the deficit, the faster our country piles up debt.
- Every Republican president since the Great Depression has left office with an unemployment rate over 5 percent (figure 2).
- Republican president Dwight D. Eisenhower holds the distinction of overseeing three recessions during his

administration. His last carried over into the Kennedy administration in 1961 (figure 1).

In figure 2 we see an up-and-down pattern. We also notice that Republican administrations correspond with periods of significantly higher unemployment. That often means more people lose their jobs during Republican administrations. The vast majority of Democratic administrations have driven unemployment down significantly. So, more Americans gain jobs during Democratic administrations.

When the economy fails, we become vulnerable to anyone, of any ideology, who promises to make things better. Sadly, our democracy might not survive such an actor. Hitler destroyed Germany and threatened the world after gaining office in an economy that had suffered a massive recession. His rise to power already showed us the danger we face in circumstances like these; we do not want to experience a similar situation again.

WHAT IS A DEFICIT?

A deficit occurs when we spend more than we earn. We have a surplus when we spend less than we earn.

The larger the deficit, the faster we accumulate debt. The smaller the deficit, the slower we accumulate debt. If we eliminate the deficit, we have not eliminated our debt; we have simply stopped accumulating more. If we lower the deficit, we have not lowered the debt or even stopped accumulating debt. When we lower the deficit, we slow down debt accumulation.

The process of eliminating our debt takes a few steps:

1. Stop growing the deficit and begin reducing it.
2. Eliminate the deficit entirely.
3. Generate a surplus.
4. Maintain that surplus until the debt is paid off.

The larger the surplus, the faster the debt disappears. Simple math. To get rid of debt, we must generate a surplus. The rules I just expressed for a deficit apply to a surplus, but in the opposite direction. The size of the surplus is directly proportional to the speed at which we pay off our debt. Every Republican administration since the Great Depression has left office with a higher deficit than when they entered office.

RECESSIONS HURT EVERYONE

Why do increased unemployment and recessions matter so much when we talk about the effectiveness of a president? Americans want to work. Our economy functions on a capitalist model. Many of us are Christians as well. The Bible tells us "if any would not work, neither should he eat."[vi] Who wants that? We find satisfaction and take pride in supporting ourselves and our families by working jobs and establishing businesses. In a capitalist economy, people must pull their own weight. Americans seem happy to do that. Recessions, at best, interrupt our ability to make that happen. At worst, they can absolutely destroy our way of life.

We live in an interdependent society. Our participation in the economy affects others within it. Each job can affect many other workers. A man with a job might buy gas to fuel his car. He might stop for breakfast at the local breakfast spot on the way to work, then later meet with friends for coffee at the local coffee shop. A working mother might employ a neighbor to watch her children after they return from school. A family might sometimes decide to go for a night out, laughing and enjoying each other's company at a local restaurant.

When a breadwinner loses their job, many of those other activities cease. The man no longer needs to stop for breakfast on the way to work, and the mother no longer needs daycare. The family can no longer afford to enjoy a night out at the local restaurant. A volunteer in an emergency room might have to get a job to help support their family now. If enough jobs are lost, businesses that supported all those working people might have to shut down. And that does not consider the family stress that job loss causes.

People tend not to make large purchases, such as automobile purchases, during recessions.[vii]

My father's auto repair business always suffered during downturns in Detroit's auto industry. Most of his customers worked in car manufacturing plants. When those plants laid off workers during recessions, his customers no longer cleaned up every scrape they discovered washing their shiny automobiles. They concerned themselves more with survival—and that meant they spent less money maintaining their beautiful cars. So my father's business, like many other businesses in Detroit, depended on the success of the auto industry.

When the economy goes into a downturn, people can lose their jobs quickly, and their lives can fall apart. Their lives can turn into a terrible storm. Someone once remarked about their unemployed father: "Unemployment might be up to 7 percent nationally, but it's 100 percent at my house."

WHEN THE ECONOMY SHRINKS, WE VOTE THEM OUT

Americans count on our government to create and execute policies that grow the economy. If a president implements policies that lead to a shrinking economy, Americans consider that president ineffective. If a president's policies lead to a growing economy, Americans consider him an effective president.

Shrinking economies have serious ramifications. A 2011 study concluded that mortality rates increase by 2.8 percent for every one percentage point rise in the unemployment rate. In shrinking economies, more people die.[viii] Another study concluded that for every one percentage point increase in the U.S. unemployment rate, we suffer thirty-seven thousand additional deaths. That's just one irreversible effect of economic downturns.

Typically, those of us caught in economic downturns suffer many negative effects. After suffering those effects, we will most likely vote to change the government. During a presidential election year, the president will lose reelection. If the president is in his second term, his party's nominee will lose. During a midterm election, the president's party will lose more seats in the House, the Senate, or both.

GROWING ECONOMY, DIFFERENT RULES

What happens when the economy is good? What happens when the economy celebrates low unemployment? When we enjoy a good job market, who do we pick? At that point, the president's party should win. After all, we punish the party that causes a shrinking economy. Fairness would suggest we reward the party that creates and sustains a growing economy. But that's not what happens.

Voters do not remember the last bad economy for very long. Most voters could not identify which president's economy spawned the last recession. They certainly could not identify which presidents raised or lowered deficits over the last decade, let alone the last century. Most people do not study the economy at that level in preparation for the next election, presidential or otherwise. Add to that a candidate willing to cover up their party's poor performance, and voters are ripe for exploitation.

Republican politicians know that their economic theory—supply-side economics—has not worked over the last century. They know that they bring about economies that shrink rather than grow. Given their history of poor economic performance (see figures 1 and 2), we should all know what to expect from Republican presidents. But we do not.

Most of us have never seen the economic evidence of how negatively Republican presidents affect our economy. Most of us do not know under which president the Great Recession started or which economic theory that president espoused. Most of us do not know that the Great Recession started under George W. Bush, which took place during most of our lifetimes, lasted longer than any recession in the previous seventy years.

We lack the focus on important economic factors necessary for selecting a president. Republican candidates can focus our attention on emotional issues that have little to do with economics. This leads many to mistakenly vote for Republicans during good economies. And, in nearly every case, we live to regret that decision, whether we admit it or not. Forgetting or getting refocused allows us to be manipulated by unsavory candidates.

How are the rules different under a good economy? Voters don't reward the party that brought about the good economy as easily as they punish the party that brought about a bad economy.

IT'S ALWAYS THE ECONOMY, STUPID

During Bill Clinton's 1992 campaign, he had a banner in his election offices that read, "It's the economy, stupid!" At the time, the unemployment rate had risen above 7 percent during the recession that started under George H. W. Bush. As the opposing party, the Democratic Party should have won the election during that shrinking economy, and they did. No problem there.

But what about in good economic times? In good economies, we do not attribute economic success to the policies of the current administration. Neither do we realize the economic risks of electing a Republican president.

After Clinton's two terms, his vice president, Al Gore, ran for office against George W. Bush. Clinton left office with an unemployment rate of 4.2 percent. Clinton was the first president since Warren G. Harding to take America's federal budget from deficit to surplus. Clinton left the economy in great shape.

But Al Gore still lost the election. The electorate did not reward Clinton's accomplishments. Some voters let their emotions get in the way again. America elected yet another supply-side advocate. And in return, Bush rewarded our lack of focus on the economy with not just one but two recessions. He also turned the $236 billion budget surplus left by Clinton into a $1.4 trillion deficit. Two of the Big Three automakers were in bankruptcy and on the verge of liquidation when Barack Obama, the next president, took office. We had allowed our focus to shift from the economy, and America paid dearly for that.

We as voters should have at the top of our minds, "It's the economy, stupid." Just like Clinton reminded his campaign staff with that banner, we should continuously remind ourselves. In growing economies, we should not allow ourselves to focus on anything else—no sleight of hand, no pulling at our heartstrings, no emotional appeals—until we have assured ourselves that we select the candidate who has a plan to keep our economy growing (rule #1). That means voting against any plan that includes supply-side economics. We should listen to any other economic plan, but not those. Nearly a century of experience has taught us that supply-side economics is always the wrong choice.

WHEN EMOTIONS DRIVE OUR POLITICS

When a presidential election takes place while the economy is growing, we assume the economy will keep growing no matter who we pick. We assume that we can choose either party's presidential candidate based on their platform and then that candidate will maintain the economy as it exists on Election Day. We believe both parties will keep the economy growing equally well. But if that were to happen, we would need two effective parties. Today, we only have one.

How do we get two effective parties?

To understand this, we first have to understand how campaigns choose what to focus on. Since our negative emotions drive us more than our positive emotions, they find issues that will generate negative emotions in their potential voters to mobilize them against their opponents. When the economy is good, it is not the source of the most powerful negative emotions, so candidates don't even address it. In the case of Republicans, they often find cultural issues to focus on.

That might not seem logical, unless we think about how emotions work. We seem to vote "I hate you" more than they vote "Thank you." What do "I hate you" and "Thank you" have in common? Both responses involve emotions—and again, negative emotions win over positive emotions when election time comes around. Whichever candidate comes up with the best "I hate you" justification wins our vote when the economy is good.

One way to stop this bad behavior on the part of the Republican Party is to never stop calling it out. Democratic candidates must help the voting public sift through the garbage and get to the point. Democrats need to have the discipline to call out the Republican Party's history of bad economies when times are good. Democrats need to warn the electorate before, during, and after elections that putting the government into the hands of Republicans has hurt the economy 100 percent of the time for nearly the last century. This is their duty as the opposing party. We, as an electorate, need the Democratic Party to do their duty.

The duration of Republicans' poor performance matters very much. Republicans can make excuses for the last administration or even the last couple of administrations, but honestly, they have nothing that will ever justify a century of recessions and high deficits. Democrat Jimmy Carter's administration sparked a recession almost fifty years ago. Since then, Republican administrations together have spawned five recessions. Each Republican administration has given rise to at least one recession.

Democrats should warn that the failing of the Republican Party has more to do with how they run the economy than anything else. Supply-side economics has always failed. Republicans keep convincing the electorate to let them try it again, but it always fails.

We as voters have the greatest responsibility; we need to vote for the correct candidates. Though candidates should point out flaws in their opponents' predecessors' performance, we voters serve as the final guard at the door. Candidates must get past us to enter office. If we fail at our jobs as citizens, we collectively cause the whole country—and in some cases, the whole world—to suffer.

SUPPLY-SIDE ECONOMICS EXIST FOR A REASON

Even though supply-side economics does not work for the entire country, it does work for the wealthy. The tax cuts promoted by supply-side economics put trillions of dollars into the pockets of the wealthiest Americans, causing them to pay a lower percentage of their income in taxes than middle-income Americans.

But supply-side economics endangers our republic. Supreme Court Justice Louis Brandeis once said, "We can have democracy in this country, or we can have great wealth concentration in the hands of a few, but we cannot have both."[ix] Brandeis pointed out that concentrating wealth in the hands of a few works counter to the goal of our republic. Since Reagan, supply-side economics has served as a great benefit to those who have worked to concentrate wealth. America's list of billionaires just keeps growing. At the same time, our Congress gets less effective. Our democracy suffers. And our national debt grows.

Conservatives convince us to vote for failed economic policy so they can continue satisfying wealthy donors who send them to Washington. The more we vote for them, the louder and more sustained the voices of their wealthiest donors will ring out. The more recessions we will see. The more wealth will concentrate. The more our national debt will increase. The more this up-and-down economic cycle will repeat. American voters are the only backstop to this cycle. This cycle will not end on its own. American voters can end supply-side economics by refusing to vote for Republicans until they change to a better economic model.

HOW SHOULD WE PICK CANDIDATES WHEN TIMES ARE GOOD?

When times are good, we must do all we can to protect the status quo. A change in administrations can hurt more than it helps. If the party that brought us 4 percent unemployment, has a problem or two, know that the party that left 6 percent, 7 percent, or 8 percent unemployment is not the source of the solution. We should pick the candidate from the party that brought about the growing economy.

The 2024 election is a great example of these principles in action. When Donald Trump left office in 2021, he left the same thing that every other Republican since the Great Depression had: unemployment over 5 percent. In fact, Trump left unemployment at 6.4 percent. When the party currently in power at the time, the Democratic party under Joe Biden, had brought unemployment down by over 35 percent to 4 percent, why would we rehire the candidate who had left office with a higher unemployment rate than when they entered office? After all, first-term Trump broke rule #1—he did not keep the economy growing. We as an electorate should not have considered Trump eligible for rehire on the general principle that he had had a chance to run the economy and he had failed.

America's choice of Trump as president a second time was particularly egregious. Not only did he belong to the party that espouses supply-side economics, but he had already failed at running the economy and lost his reelection after his first term. The country knew that Trump had already left the largest annual budget deficit in American history—$2.7 trillion—when he left office. And, in addition to all that, under Trump's administration, the economy suffered a net job loss for the first time since the Great Depression. America chose a president who had already failed at running the economy from a party that routinely fails at running the economy.

So, even though Republicans bring about shrinking economies and lose, they produce enough negative emotions about Democrats during good economies to win again. And even though Democrats win in bad economies and bring the economy back from recession, they lose after those important successes. Democrats don't inspire enough positive emotions about their economic success, and they also fail to frame Republican economic failures in a way that generates strong negative emotions. If I did not understand the emotional element of elections, I would think that Americans participate in a decision that mimics collective self-harm. During good economies we decide to hire proven economy abusers.

In Iowa, during the 2024 presidential election, Trump only lost five of Iowa's ninety-nine counties. He won the five largest farming counties. Farmers voted overwhelmingly for Trump.

Farmers had suffered under Trump's first administration, but they were doing better after Trump's bailout during his first term. Their marginal success lasted through Joe Biden's term. After Biden's term, farmers felt more comfortable with the Republican Party, so they voted for Trump again, even though he signaled the possibility of a trade war with China, one of their largest customers. In the process, they voted themselves into a financial nightmare.

Iowa farmers did not consider how both parties had historically affected their farm economy. They assumed that the economy they were experiencing on Election Day 2024 would continue, no matter who they selected. Since things had gotten marginally better for them, they gave both candidates equal stature. Then they selected their preference based on current feelings—a Republican.

Since they did not consider the history of our economy under the recent Republican candidate, they left themselves open to the negative effects of another economic downturn. And sure enough, shortly after Trump began his second term, he imposed worldwide tariffs. The new tariffs caused many of the farmers' export partners to stop buying their crops. As their trading partners' relationships with the United States government deteriorated, they lost those markets to other countries.

Farmer's top export destinations—Canada, Mexico, and China—all bought less. Trump put massive tariffs on all three countries on what the Trump Administration called Liberation Day, April 2, 2025. Trump refused to honor the agreement he signed with Canada and Mexico during his first term, the United States–Mexico–Canada Agreement (USMCA).

Trump responded with a partial bailout—but farmers did not want a bailout. Every businessperson would rather have a functioning market than a government bailout. Farmers wanted the administration to allow the international market for their products to stand as it had during the previous administration. Farmers had ideas for improving relationships and expanding international markets for their products. Tariff increases were not among those ideas. Trump's policies caused a rise in farm bankruptcies by 46 percent in 2025.[x]

Though tariffs caused most of the damage, other decisions made by the Trump administration hurt farmers as well. By the end of Trump's first month in office, he ordered a review of all U.S. foreign assistance programs. By the end of July, he canceled nearly all contracts administered by the United States Agency for International Development (USAID). Many American farmers had substantial contracts with USAID to grow and ship food to developing countries worldwide. Some farmers grow crops solely to supply USAID contracts. When those contracts ended, those farmers had no other business.

Farmers undoubtedly voted on issues that concerned them. But their plight under the Trump administration shows that economic interests must always remain front of mind. We cannot let our feelings or votes override our needs.

When the economy is strong, we have abundant employment, the dollar rises against foreign currencies, the government collects substantial revenue, and, under the right administration, the country borrows less. If we wish to get our country out of debt, we must focus and make the right decisions about which candidates to support during elections, especially in good economic times.

When we allow ourselves to depart from the idea that the American economy matters more than anything else the government can do to impact our lives, we risk financial ruin. Republicans sell Americans on the idea that cultural issues should matter more to us than anything else. We only learn otherwise when we find ourselves having to endure a bad economy after another electoral mistake.

When times are good, we must maintain focus on keeping the economy growing. Economic growth must rank right at the top of our list of criteria for selecting a new or existing administration. If any candidate is not keenly focused on growing the economy and, thereby, jobs and exports, we should reject them without a second thought. We don't need them to preach to us about social issues. We have other places to reconcile those matters.

HOW DO WE GET TWO EFFECTIVE PARTIES?

Today, we reward two things by voting for Republicans. First, we reward their failed job performance in running the economy. They know they preside over the worst economic crises. Higher unemployment rates, higher deficits, lower job creation numbers, and lower GDP numbers—all resound the "bad economy" story quite well. Republicans cannot fool us on that. As we have shown, our economy under Republican presidents performs poorly. We can see that in the unemployment and recession data. Second, we reward their ingenuity for getting us to vote for them by provoking emotions against their opponents during good economies.

Remember, insanity is doing the same thing repeatedly and expecting a different result each time. When pursuing supply-side economics, our government has consistently delivered indisputably negative economic results, so at this point, it would be insanity to expect their supply-side approach to produce a different result. Until Republicans prove to the American voter that they are not insane, they should never have a majority in the House nor the Senate, and we certainly should not elect a Republican as president again. If a Republican candidate leads with tax cuts when America has a $39 trillion debt, we should assume the candidate has not shaken off that form of insanity. We should not elect another Republican until they ensure us that they will not try the same approach again. That supply-side approach to economics has never worked for our country.

WHAT WILL IT TAKE TO MAKE CHANGE?

What will it take for us to hold both parties equally accountable for successfully running our economy? In 1929, it took the collapse of the stock market, the banks, and the economy overall before we made serious change. Many Americans had lost their homes. They formed communities of tent homes and called those communities Hoovervilles. Perhaps we must lose it all again before we realize the importance of our electoral choices.

After Herbert Hoover, we did not elect another Republican president for twenty-four years. Perhaps that's just how America works. We do not realize what we have when times are good. We only realize what we had after we lose it.

I would hope that time and history have made us smarter than that. There was no guarantee that Franklin D. Roosevelt could restore our country's economy after the Great Depression. He realized that. He took the economy seriously. Roosevelt saw our economic struggles as an existential threat to our country. Whether we see that now or not, it's still the truth.

We can start making the change by detaching our emotions from our votes. Many of us get fooled into voting one way or another over emotional issues. For instance, many of us who are Christians think that somehow the Republican Party represents our religious values because they call themselves "Conservatives" and we have conservative moral values. Not true. We need to discover for ourselves the truth of what they mean before we credit them with both and give them our votes. A religiously conservative organization would not advocate for an immoral leader.

We can understand this idea better once we understand what we actually mean when we use the labels "Liberal" and "Conservative."

CHAPTER 2
WHAT ARE CONSERVATIVES?

> *I don't want to abolish government. I simply want to reduce it to the size where I can drag it into the bathroom and drown it in the bathtub."*
>
> GROVER NORQUIST

WHO WOULD CONSIDER THEMSELVES "A CONSERVATIVE"?

MANY PEOPLE who consider themselves Conservatives in the political sense are not. The word "conservative" describes a philosophy or an action. When we use the term "a Conservative," we are using a shortcut in English—we are saying "a conservative person." But that phrase alone lacks the detail necessary for us to understand what about this person we consider conservative.

We understand that "a Conservative" is a person. We also understand that something about that person is conservative. We do not, however, understand what attribute, behavior, or philosophy about that person is conservative.

We call that shortcut in English nominalization. We use nominalization all the time. If I said, "I like sweets," people would assume I'm talking about food. I'm not talking about sweet cars or sweet jump shots in basketball. In this case, everyone understands when I say, "I like sweets," I mean food with a high sugar content like cake or candy.

We can use the word "sweet" to describe many things. She is a sweet person. Those bananas are sweet. That is a sweet car. But when I use the shortcut "sweets," I do not have to add "foods" to the sentence —I can say, "I like sweets," and everyone understands that I mean "I like foods with high sugar content." They know that I do not mean foods that are generally sweet like bananas. They understand that I mean foods high in sugar, like candy, cake, or donuts. That's how nominalization works.

In American politics, we use "a Conservative" or "Conservatives" in the same way. But not everyone understands exactly what being "a Conservative" means. We do understand that a Conservative is a person, but beyond that, we do not necessarily understand much else about that person.

That's a problem. If society does not understand a word used as a shortcut, that designation means nothing to society. Dishonest people can then change its meaning to anything that suits their purpose. Since one person's understanding of the attributes of a Conservative can differ greatly from another's, the phrase "a Conservative" used to describe a person tells us nothing about that person.

Many people who think they are Conservatives in the political sense really are not. Some mix in various conservative ideas under that designation. If they want "a Conservative" to mean a person possessing fiscally conservative economic philosophy, it can mean that. If they want "a Conservative" to mean a person who lives a religiously moral lifestyle, it can mean that. Heck, if they want "a Conservative" to mean a person who is so socially skeptical that he has a hard time dealing with other people, it can mean that. But there is no general understanding as to which conservative feature or philosophy we should ascribe to people when they call themselves Conservatives.

That leaves the interpretation of the phrase "a Conservative" wide open. When we leave a term's meaning wide open, it means nothing. It could also mean anything. As we might imagine, Republicans want us to think we are all Conservatives at election time. Of course, the more people who think they are Conservatives, the better the chances Republican candidates have of winning their elections.

Because the term "a Conservative" does not tell us much about a person, "a political Conservative" does not tell us anything either. Well, it does tell us, in today's American political environment, that the person probably belongs to the Republican Party. But it does not tell us much about what they believe.

Attempting to determine what the term "conservative" has meant over time led me on a journey to understand what makes a Conservative, well, conservative. Why would someone call themselves a Conservative? What should that label mean to me and to other Americans?

At the time, I asked myself, "What have I missed?" Had I missed something in history that would have made the answers to my questions obvious? Did everyone else understand something I had completely overlooked? What did Americans generally understand? But then I thought, "If its meaning is generally understood, I would understand it."

The word's lack of a clearly understood meaning is as dangerous in politics as an open manhole cover on a sidewalk. If we are not paying attention, we can fall in. And if one of us falls in, they could be injured or killed. The same is true of the "Conservative" designation: falling into it without understanding what it means can be dangerous, politically and economically.

WHAT ABOUT MORALITY?

I discovered through my personal experience that people who claim to be Conservatives are not necessarily religiously moral. In fact, many politicians who call themselves Conservatives are quite accomplished liars and even criminals, like Richard Nixon and Donald Trump. The Republican Party—the party of Conservatives—has shown itself to be unwilling to reject these liars and criminals, which contradicts its claims to be a party of religiously moral people or a party of law and order.

Jimmy Carter had a reputation for teaching Bible classes in Washington, D.C., while he served as president. He regularly attended Sunday services at the First Baptist Church there. After leaving office, he taught Bible classes at the Maranatha Baptist Church in Plains, Georgia, well into his nineties. He only stopped teaching Bible classes when his health began to fail a few years before his death at one hundred years old. People who knew Carter considered him a faithful man with high moral values. His marriage—his only marriage—to Rosalynn Carter lasted seventy-seven years until she died. That lifestyle and those values may sound "conservative" to you, but Carter considered himself a Liberal. Just as a person who calls himself a Conservative does not necessarily have religious moral values, a person who calls himself a Liberal does not necessarily lack those values.

In the history of our country, only two presidents won election to office after divorcing and remarrying: Ronald Reagan and Donald Trump (Trump remarried twice). They both consider themselves Conservatives. I'm a Christian who knows the Bible, and neither would have qualified for church leadership according to the Bible.[i] So "a Conservative" could not universally mean a person who holds conservative Christian morals.

That's not to say that we hold presidents to the same standards as church leaders. We do not and have not. But some of us remember a time in America when a man who cheated on his wife and divorced her could not win an election anywhere, ever again. That time has passed.

In the history of our country, no presidential candidate had ever been indicted of a single felony by any court, state, or federal before Trump ran for a second term in 2024. When Trump ran, he had been indicted of multiple felonies in multiple jurisdictions. Only one president has been impeached twice. Only one presidential candidate has ever been indicted of a felony by the federal Department of Justice. The candidate with this lengthy criminal rap sheet, Donald Trump, still won the 2024 Republican presidential nomination and the presidency.

As far as the party of Conservatives, the Republican Party, is concerned, a candidate can live a low moral life and even be convicted of a crime, yet still comfortably fit within that party. So being a Conservative does not mean they have to adhere to the principles of law and order. Nor does it mean they must live a life that takes a conservative view of lawbreaking.

WHAT ABOUT FISCAL POLICY?

Do Republicans have a record of conservative fiscal policy and practice? Do they spend our nation's tax revenue carefully and reduce our debt when given the opportunity of a good economy? The answer is no. Not only do they not have a record of conservative fiscal policy and practice, but administrations of Conservatives have practiced reckless spending.

Every Republican administration since the Great Depression has left office with a larger annual budget deficit than when it entered office. We must understand that the higher the budget deficit, the faster our nation accumulates debt.

Ronald Reagan	1981–1989	8 years	+94%
George H.W. Bush	1989-1993	4 years	+67%
Bill Clinton	1993-2001	8 years	-150%
George W. Bush	2001–2009	8 years	+64%
Barack Obama	2009–2017	8 years	-53%
Donald Trump	2017–2021	4 years	+317%
Joe Biden	2021–2025	4 years	-35%

Figure 3: Amount Presidents increase/decreased the deficit since 1989 (*A-Mark Foundation U.S. Presidents and the Federal Deficit - February 3, 2023*)

Figure 3 shows the amount that each president since Ronald Reagan has raised or lowered the annual budget deficit. In the table, we see each president, the date range of their tenure, their years in office, and the percentage they raised or lowered the federal budget deficit. Notice that every Democratic president significantly reduced the deficit, while every Republican president significantly increased it.

The last Republican president that reduced the budget deficit by the time they left office was Calvin Coolidge. Most of us do not remember Coolidge. Most of our grandparents would not remember him. Coolidge left office almost a century ago.

To reduce our national debt, a presidential administration would have to wipe out the budget deficit, create a budget surplus, and then use that surplus to pay off debt over several years. Only one president since Coolidge has done that. Bill Clinton left office in 2001 with a $236 billion budget surplus after eight years in office. Clinton is a Liberal, but he exercised fiscally responsible policy. Clinton raised taxes and cut spending to keep his campaign promise to balance the budget.

No matter what Republican candidates have said during their campaigns, by and large, they have not delivered fiscally responsible policy while in office during my lifetime. Republicans have not reduced the annual federal budget deficit, let alone balanced the budget, though they have produced plenty of rhetoric claiming they would. Republicans seem to introduce balanced budget amendments to the Constitution nearly every term. But in Congress and in the White House, they increase the deficit nearly every term. So, we could not universally understand "a Conservative" to mean a person with a fiscally conservative philosophy.

WHAT ABOUT SPENDING?

The federal government did not shrink in size or spending under any Republican administration during my lifetime. Every one of them made government larger, not smaller, in all cases in spending and in many cases in size. George W. Bush added the Department of Homeland Security and started multi-trillion dollar wars. Donald Trump added an entirely new branch to the military called the Space Force and started a war with Iran. Given this history, "a Conservative" could not mean a person who aspired to reduce the size of the government. I'm not judging their decisions—I'm just observing them.

Using deductive reasoning, we can reach clear, straightforward conclusions. To understand something, we can rule out various components that we discover are not part of it. If we continue using that process, we will eventually come to understand what that thing is.

So far, most of the conservative philosophies Conservatives attribute to the Republican Party are misplaced. But they must be conservative about something, or else they would not call themselves Conservatives—right? Their use of the label must mean that they believe in some conservative philosophy. Let's keep digging.

SO, LET'S KEEP GOING BACK

I kept going back. I went from Reagan to Nixon to Eisenhower, and then I went back even further, even before the Great Depression. I never quite saw a thread that suggested moral values, conservative spending, or conservative fiscal policy in the federal government by Conservatives as universally understood traits. Conservatives certainly did not universally practice those things.

I had to go back to the Civil War to begin to understand Conservatives. Looking at the Civil War, I got a better understanding of Conservatives and Liberals. But, I realized, to get a complete understanding, I had to go back even further, to the writing of the Constitution.

That takes us back to the year 1787. I found a foundational understanding of Conservatives and Liberals in American history at that unlikely time. I first noticed people calling each other "Conservatives" and "Liberals" back then.

THE ARTICLES OF CONFEDERATION DID NOT WORK

The United States of America operated under the Articles of Confederation and Perpetual Union as its first constitution. The founders of our nation drafted the Articles of Confederation in 1776 during the Revolutionary War, and it was signed as their constitution in 1777. The United States and Great Britain signed the Treaty of Paris, ending the Revolutionary War, in 1783. The United States operated under the Articles of Confederation during the Revolutionary War and for around five years after the Treaty of Paris.

Under the Articles of Confederation, the Continental Congress made up the entire federal government. Representatives from each state gathered to comprise the Continental Congress. No matter the population, landmass, or value of a given state, each state only got one vote on matters decided by the Continental Congress. There was no standing army. There was no Supreme Court. There was only the Continental Congress.

The Continental Congress wrote and passed laws. The Continental Congress also appointed judges to settle disputes among and between the states.

Each year, the Continental Congress appointed a president. But the president had only a ceremonial role to play in the government. He served as president over the "Committee of the States." The president had no real power and could only serve for that one year. We had eight such presidents over the Continental Congress before we elected George Washington under the Constitution.

The United States had many problems under the Articles of Confederation. America incurred significant debt during the Revolutionary War. Many states did not pay their fair share in taxes—if they paid any taxes at all. States even had wars with each other. Some states signed treaties with other countries. Under the Articles of Confederation, the country did not operate as a unified nation of states. The federal government was very weak.

Most of the states had problems with how the country operated under that constitution. So, they voted to change how the country worked by changing their constitution. The Continental Congress, with the permission of the states, called a constitutional convention to make the Articles of Confederation work better.

So, what does this have to do with Conservatives? Stay with me here.

THE STATES CREATED THE U.S. CONSTITUTION

Each state appointed representatives to the Constitutional Convention in Philadelphia, scheduled for May of 1787. They met to propose changes to the Articles of Confederation to help the country operate more effectively. However, after months of deliberation, the convention decided to throw out the Articles of Confederation and to instead write an entirely new constitution with a completely different structure. That document was to become the United States Constitution.

The Constitutional Convention of 1787 finished the completely new U.S. Constitution on September 17, 1787. The requisite number of states ratified it by June of 1788. The Constitution then replaced the Articles of Confederation as our nation's constitution.

The Constitution was drastically different from the Articles of Confederation. The Constitution established three branches of government: the executive, legislative, and judicial branches. The president of the United States is the head of the executive branch. The legislative branch consists of Congress, which has two houses: the House of Representatives and the Senate. The judicial branch includes the Supreme Court, with sitting justices nominated by the president and confirmed by the Senate. The Constitution also established a standing army and navy.

Altogether, the Constitutional Convention that met in Philadelphia in May through September of 1787 established a strong central government. This new government looked nothing like the weak federal government they had met to fix.

That new government structure created serious problems.

THE NEW CONSTITUTION CREATED CONFLICT

From that point forward, there was conflict among politicians over whether we should have continued with the Articles of Confederation or established a new, stronger central government through the Constitution. That decision became the dividing line between Conservatives and Liberals.

Liberals believed that this new, more powerful, federal government would help America accomplish great things. Conservatives believed that the central government should not, in practice, exist. Conservatives believed that a powerful central government would dictate too much to the states. Conservatives also believed that the states should have the power to do whatever pleased them. The Articles of Confederation laid out the relationship between the states using the following language:

> *Article III. The said states hereby severally enter into a firm league of friendship with each other.*

The United States Constitution does not characterize the relationship between the states as loosely as a "league of friendship." The Constitution completely intertwined the states in the new central government. Citizens, rather than states, could pay taxes. And unlike the old government, the new government had the power to enforce tax collection. The new government could pass laws by which all states had to live. The Constitution made the laws created by the federal government the "supreme law of the land." The new government could enforce those laws with its own judiciary.

This point of separation—a weak and ineffective federal government versus a strong federal government—became the dividing line between Liberals and Conservatives. Conservatives wanted to go back to the Articles of Confederation. Liberals embraced the U.S. Constitution.

THE CIVIL WAR FURTHER DIVIDED LIBERALS AND CONSERVATIVES

This conflict between Conservatives and Liberals stewed and thickened over the next seventy years. It went on through the Northwest Indian War, the War of 1812, the Mexican–American War, and finally the American Civil War.

I discuss the Civil War as a war between two countries. That description fits. Others describe the opponents as the Union and the Confederacy. To me, that sounds like two parts of the same country. It sounds a bit whitewashed. For the brief four-year period in which the Civil War took place, the battle raged between two countries, the United States of America (USA) and the Confederate States of America (CSA). The states of the CSA left our country to form their own country. They wrote their own constitution; they elected a president and a Congress. The CSA also had its own currency.

Jefferson Davis, a former senator from Mississippi, served as the president of the CSA for the entire existence of that country. Davis wrote a book that details the cause of the war, the war itself, and its outcome from his perspective.

In Davis's book, *The Rise and Fall of the Confederate Government*, Davis begins part I, the first ten chapters of the first volume, by discussing slavery as part of the cause. After all, every state that joined that country after seceding from the United States of America, and listed causes, had slavery as the primary cause or a major cause for their secession. Each state that seceded (left the United States) called a secession convention. During these conventions, each legislature agreed to secede. Each legislature then wrote a "Declaration of Secession" or a similar document. That document declared that state's separation from the United States. It also explained their reasons for separation. In nearly all these documents, states mentioned their fear of the demise of slavery as their principal reason for leaving.

However, in the next fifteen chapters of part II of the first volume of his book, Davis discusses the writing of the Constitution. At first, that seemed odd to me. How could the Constitution play into the cause of the Civil War? Davis explains that the Constitutional Convention should only have revised the Articles of Confederation. He believed that the representatives sent by each state did not, as a body, have the authority to completely restructure the country's government. Davis also thought the Constitution created a wedge between southern states and the federal government.

Davis writes exhaustively about how the Constitution came about, including the problems and divisions the country encountered when it replaced the Articles of Confederation with the Constitution. Davis also writes about the many problems he had with the Constitution.

Confederates saw the government created by the Constitution as the cause of division between major American political ideologies. Many Confederates saw the Constitution as creating a government much like the one the United States had left in England. They saw the president as an imperial leader. They saw the central government as a potentially oppressive organization, especially to the states.

Just as slavery lay quietly under the table as the Constitution took form, it became the backstory of this conflict between those who thought of the new government as a masterpiece and those who feared the new government as a big mistake.

Davis called the people who thought the Constitution a masterpiece Liberals. He called those who saw the new constitution as a threat Conservatives.

When I think about it, this aligns with my understanding of the term "conservative." The Conservatives wanted to preserve the old constitution and its government structure. The Liberals wanted to progress from something that did not work to something that would serve as a foundation for further progress.

When I read *The Rise and Fall of Confederate Government,* Davis did not lay out Liberal and Conservative terminology and ideology that plainly. I deduced his definition from what he implied. He called his allies "conservatives," and he called those who thought otherwise and voted otherwise "liberals."

The southern states seemed always weary and guarded about the northern states and their desire to abolish slavery—so much so that once Abraham Lincoln won the 1860 election, South Carolina, the first state to separate from the United States of America, left over two months before Lincoln ever even took office.

Modern-day Confederate sympathizers have complained about all the things Lincoln did to cause their ancestors to secede. But Lincoln had not yet entered office when the CSA formed and their states began to secede from the USA.

CONFEDERATES WERE THE FIRST CONSERVATIVES

As I was explaining how the Constitution came about, some would probably draw a connection between the Confederate States of America and the Articles of Confederation. They do have a word in common: "Confederate."

Perhaps some would expect that when these people, who did not like the idea of the new United States Constitution, formed their own government, they would return to the Articles of Confederation as their constitution. After all, they called their new government a confederate government.

The Articles of Confederation described the government as a "league of friendship" among independent states, creating the impression that membership was non-binding. Conservatives believed states could participate if they wanted or leave if they wanted. The Constitution, on the other hand, included much more specific language, binding each state with no clear way to leave.

When Abraham Lincoln won the 1860 election, Republicans—the party of Liberals at the time—also won the House of Representatives and the Senate. The Democrats—the party of Conservatives back then—feared that Lincoln and the houses of Congress controlled by Liberals would pass legislation to abolish slavery immediately. So, the slaveholding states in the South seceded from the United States of America. They left the USA and formed the CSA.

Lincoln would take office on March 4, 1861. By the time Lincoln took office, the CSA had seceded from the USA, written a constitution, established a Congress, issued currency, and elected a provisional president, Jefferson Davis. Davis took his oath of office on February 18, 1861. That's right—Jefferson Davis took office before Abraham Lincoln.

When the CSA established their new government, they wrote a constitution that was quite similar to the U.S. Constitution. It differed in several ways, including their philosophy toward slavery and in the tenure of each president, which they set at six years. The CSA organized its government substantially the same way the United States had.

Strangely, though, they called themselves the Confederate States of America when they used a structure that made their central government stronger than the central government of the Articles of Confederation. I speculate that this was because they knew that the government setup under the Articles of Confederation did not work. Many of their leaders, including Jefferson Davis, their president, had served in different roles in the United States government. As mentioned previously, Davis had served as a U.S. senator from Mississippi.

And even though the CSA organized under a nearly identical constitution, the states' rights philosophy of confederation overwhelmed their federal government's ability to govern its states. In fact, by the end of the Civil War, Davis demanded that the CSA's states work together more effectively. Davis thought that, as president, he should have the same power as Abraham Lincoln.

Davis realized that confederation did not work as a governing philosophy. When he had big things to accomplish—namely, to win the war for their survival—he needed more centralized power, resources, and cooperation among the states. By 1865, it was too late.

The idea of a nation comprised of a confederation of states made the CSA comfortable that each of the slave states would keep their slaves. They had confidence, based on that idea and their constitution. Their ability to keep an economy based on slavery was no longer in jeopardy. But it did not work. Weak, disorganized governments do not work.

CONSERVATIVES DESIRE A WEAKER FEDERAL GOVERNMENT

Based on my retrospective on Conservatives, we have observed what seems to be the only generalizable understanding of "a Conservative." We understand that a Conservative is someone who would prefer the federal government to be as weak and powerless as possible. The only exception to that rule is the military. Conservatives want a strong military. But they want weak legislative, executive, and judicial branches of the federal government. Conservatives would rather each state make its own decisions, unfettered by federal law. For Conservatives, states' rights should rule the day.

Grover Norquist, a Conservative and activist, made this statement during a May 25, 2001, interview with NPR when talking about the $1.5 trillion George W. Bush federal tax cuts:

> *I don't want to abolish government. I simply want to reduce it to the size where I can drag it into the bathroom and drown it in the bathtub."*[ii]

Norquist expresses the same sentiment that Jefferson Davis did in his book 140 years earlier. This is the same sentiment Ronald Reagan expressed thirty years prior when he said, "Government is the problem"[iii] during the 1980 presidential election.

This small government understanding of Conservatives holds up. Conservatives want a small and weak federal government, akin to the government the Articles of Confederation created at our nation's inception. Conservatives only advocate for moral values and conservative fiscal policy during elections and during political fights. But history shows us that they do not govern—or even live—that way.

The consistent thread that runs through the governing philosophies of Conservatives, as I've observed them, is a weak federal government. This philosophy has remained consistent from the writing of the Articles of Confederation until today.

Donald Trump nearly abolished the Department of Education in 2025, cutting its budget over $200 billion. Trump nearly abolished USAID in 2025. Same idea. Same thread of thought. Conservatives' goal is to squeeze the federal government at every turn. Their policies, once they are in office, bear that out.

During a closed event in April 2026, Trump said (referring to Iran War funding), "It's not possible for us to take care of daycare, Medicaid, Medicare...We have to take care of one thing, military protection."[iv]

CONSERVATIVES' IDEAS CAN BE REGRESSIVE

The word "conservative," by its very definition, calls us to look back in time because whatever someone claims they want to conserve must already exist. When something already exists, it came into being in the past. It is only possible to conserve or preserve something that originated in the past.

We have many practices and values we want to preserve. I personally count Christian moral values among those. I mark as sacred God's law, rule, and practice and want to preserve them unaltered by the modern understandings of men.

Governments, the Christian faith teaches, are ordained by God. However, they are set up by and staffed by people. We hope those people establish governments based on their best understanding as to how a citizenry can safely work together and prosper. I see America's constitutional republic as being among the best, but make no mistake, God did not write the Constitution. The Constitution is a fallible document. The Constitution is a document written by men.

In fact, the Framers of the Constitution wrote Article V into that document. Article V allows amendments to the Constitution. The Framers had enough intelligence to understand that the document they wrote would eventually need to change. The Constitution lays out a great structure for government, but it is not perfect.

Unlike systems inspired by God, systems created by people must change. They must progress. Their structures, to the extent that they serve their citizens, should remain in place. But progress demands that the substance changes.

Sometimes governments change because modern inventions require new approaches. Sometimes they change because the citizenry discovers that the founders did not deal correctly with an issue that existed in their time. And sometimes they must change because more capable people grasp the reins of power and convince the people that our systems need refreshing to move the country forward.

Liberals and Conservatives should struggle with progress versus the status quo. That struggle should cause a fair amount of deliberation and intellectual sparring. But these days, our politicians have gotten caught up in expressing their opinions and philosophies as right and wrong. Rather than taking on opponents and proving their point, Conservatives seem to want to disqualify their opponents based on legal and moral grounds.

MANY CONSERVATIVES HAVE LIBERAL PERSONAL VALUES

Conservatives can have low moral values. That's certainly not to say that Conservatives share Liberals' values; Liberals and low moral values are two different things.

The Manhattan District Attorney won convictions in a jury trial on thirty-four counts against Trump for falsifying business documents.[v] Trump lost two lawsuits against E. Jean Carroll over defamation allegations.[vi] The defamation suits stemmed from Trump calling Carroll a liar when she accused Trump of sexual assault. She had to prove in court, under oath, that she had told the truth when she accused Trump of sexually assaulting her.

After those thirty-four felony convictions in Manhattan, along with other indictments that were never tried and two successfully adjudicated sexual assault-related lawsuits, Trump won reelection to the office of president of the United States. Conservatives were willing to set aside Trump's loose morals, values, and choices in favor of the political beliefs they felt they had in common with him. They did not care about his lack of religious moral values. They knew that Trump played golf on Sunday morning when many people attend worship services.

The Republican Party's portion of the electorate looked the other way or decided jury convictions were not enough to sway their belief in Trump as the leader of the party of Conservatives. They watched Trump tell lie after lie on live television and on social media. Conservatives did not care about moral values because being a Conservative does not mean they possess moral values.

Other Conservatives do not believe in conservative personal values. Log Cabin Republicans, as they call themselves, are gay people who believe in the small government values of Republicans. They are Conservatives. They also stand as witnesses to the fact that Conservatives are not necessarily religiously conservative.

CONSERVATIVES LEAD WITH THEIR IDEOLOGY

Now we should understand that Conservatives have a single thing in common: They believe in a small, weak federal government. Because they think the federal government cannot do much right, they believe we should rely on state governments and private businesses for policy and its execution.

The Affordable Care Act (ACA) went into full force in 2014. Barack Obama signed it into law in 2010. At the time of this writing in 2026, although Republicans have railed against the plan, they have yet to come up with a comprehensive replacement.

During the 2024 presidential campaign, when the press asked Donald Trump about his plan to replace the ACA, he promised that he had "concepts of a plan."[vii] Yet even though Republicans have controlled the legislative and executive branches since Trump took office, Republicans have yet to pass a single healthcare replacement plan in either house, let alone get one to the president's desk for signature.

Some might think I am mentioning this ACA problem as a final jab in the ribs of Conservatives. Definitely not. I mention it to make a very important point.

Republicans have complained about the ACA since it passed, but they have not put forward a viable healthcare plan to replace the ACA. They have had more than fifteen years since the ACA was first signed into law. That should tell us something. Republicans have introduced and voted on legislation to kill the ACA over fifty times. In 2017, the ACA survived by a single vote when John McCain voted against its repeal in the Senate, after the House of Representatives had passed the repeal. Those actions send a clear signal.

What should those actions help us realize? They should help us to understand that Conservatives do not want the federal government to do anything about healthcare. No matter how poorly our current health insurance system works for Americans, the overriding philosophy of Conservatives will win out when they hold power. Conservatives do not believe that health insurance should be the business of government. Apart from national defense, Conservatives would rather the government not get involved, especially in a program as large as government-subsidized health insurance. They would rather the private sector solve all problems that we as citizens encounter. That's an attribute of the ideology of Conservatives.

I'm using the ACA as an example because private companies have bastardized our healthcare system. In their effort to make it profitable, they have reduced care for some and eliminated it for others. Private companies in the healthcare sector do not exist to keep us healthy; they exist to make a profit. That's the reason any private company exists. I understand that. I have owned a company, like my father before me did, for decades.

We cannot count on private companies to help us out of the goodness of their hearts. Companies do not have hearts. We cannot expect compassion from them. They are not people. Again, they exist to make a profit for their investors—as well they should.

Herein lies the paradox of conservatism. Our federal government cannot be a government "of the people, by the people, for the people,"[viii] as Abraham Lincoln characterized it, if we elect people who do not believe in its possibilities but rather only believe in their rigid ideologies. Our government will not accomplish much if the people who run it disdain the government itself. Our government's potential gets stifled by rigid ideologies.

Republicans will just string us along—in this case spending over a decade and a half knowing full well that they will never come up with a new healthcare plan. Because coming up with a healthcare plan goes against their ideology. The prospect of eliminating government-run health insurance is not very attractive to poor and middle-income Americans, especially those with pre-existing health conditions. So, Conservatives will promise to do something that they never plan to do. If they told the truth about their ideology during elections,

Conservatives fear that they would lose, so they must sell voters something else. Conservatives must sell emotion.

CONCLUSION

We asked, "What are Conservatives?" Conservatives value a limited federal government. But they go farther than that. They disdain the power of our federal government. They would rather see that power greatly reduced.

For some people—people who believe America, all of America, is everything it should be right now—that's fine. But for those who believe we have real work to do, the ideology of Conservatives does not work. Whether or not any of us agree with that ideology is a political determination that each person must make.

But be clearheaded about the ideology of Conservatives. It's not religious, fiscal, or any other conservative philosophy some might attach to the Republican Party. Those voters who believe that the federal government should be so weak that someone could drag it into the bathroom and drown it in the bathtub, as Grover Norquist put it, are Conservatives. Those who believe Reagan's philosophy that "the nine most frightening words in the English language are 'I'm from the government and I'm here to help,'"[ix] those are Conservatives. Those who do not should perhaps reconsider the use of that label.

Let me offer one last bit of advice. Even if you are someone who believes in conservatism, who believes the federal government should be weak and feckless—voting for candidates from the Republican Party should still be something that you do with great thought and discernment.

The Republican Party may be the party you desire. It might share your ideology. But in the party's current state, the Republican Party damages our economy, causing millions of Americans to suffer. Execution of their ideology always causes our economy to go into recession—always.

So, I offer this: Pick smart candidates to support. Don't just pick any Republican. If you do plan to pick a Republican, make sure that candidate does not buy into supply-side economics. The last one hundred years of trying to implement that ideology have failed and failed miserably. Make sure the candidates you pick will use a better economic philosophy.

However you vote, vote with a level head. Don't get dragged into emotional issues and vote on them. Instead, vote for reasoned, competent, moral people who will govern the economy in a way that will cause it to grow.

CHAPTER 3
WHAT ARE LIBERALS?

> *But the Constitution is not the Bible—far from it. The Framers of the Constitution dedicated an entire article to explain how to amend or change that man-made document."*

WHO WOULD CONSIDER THEMSELVES "A LIBERAL"?

NOW THAT WE understand what we mean when we call a person "a Conservative" and some of the history behind that, we can better understand what we mean when we call a person "a Liberal."

Politically, Liberals believe nearly the opposite of what Conservatives believe about the federal government. We believe that the federal government can accomplish great things when all of its parts work in concert. We believe we should not cede more power to the federal government than the Constitution affords it. But as Liberals —and this is especially true for Black Liberals—we know that a weak and feckless federal government does not work well and does not accomplish much for us. We understand that a federal government that overpowers its citizens could do harm more than good. We need the right balance. We know that a growing economy is the root of all progress.

LIBERALS WANT PROGRESS

Liberals concern themselves more with progress. Many Liberals even call themselves progressives. They do not see the Constitution as secular scripture, but more as a framework for a government "of the people, for the people, by the people," as Abraham Lincoln described it. When I say they see the Constitution as a "framework," I do not mean that they believe they can ignore any part of it.

In fact, Liberals believe that the Constitution, as the drafters designed it, sets up a framework with which we can create a society that should operate as a fair and equitable republic.

The words "liberal" and "progressive" look to the future. They look for the possible more than the past. Black people have needed "progress" since the inception of this country. Black people absolutely could not remain in the same space we occupied in America when our founders wrote the Constitution. If we had, we would still be enslaved people. We required progress to come as far as we have. Even with all the progress America has made, we need our country to keep moving forward.

Liberals in government have worked to provide needed progress. After the Civil War began and raged on for a year and a half, Lincoln took private time away from the fight. He traveled to the Soldiers' Home about three miles north of the White House to write the Emancipation Proclamation. He would introduce the Preliminary Emancipation Proclamation on September 22, 1862. The final emancipation of slaves in the CSA states took place on January 1, 1863.

Lincoln knew that the Emancipation Proclamation could not stand for all time. After all, the Emancipation Proclamation was a presidential executive order. Conservatives could quickly rescind that executive order as soon as they gained control of the presidency. So, Lincoln advocated for the Thirteenth Amendment to the Constitution. That amendment would abolish slavery in the United States for all time. Liberals also delivered the Fourteenth and Fifteenth

Amendments for Black people. We needed their help to keep making progress.

Enslaved people got freedom, the right of citizenship, and the right to vote because Liberals in government did the work necessary to make those rights possible. Black people were powerless to help bring these changes about because of slavery. But an effective federal government worked to overcome the bondage we suffered in many of this country's states.

In the mid-1900s, the Supreme Court decision Brown v. the Board of Education of Topeka, Kansas, and legislative accomplishments championed by Liberals such as the Civil Rights Act, the Voting Rights Act, and the Fair Housing Act brought about more of the progress we as Black people needed in modern America.

Liberal judges and legislators pushed through those decisions and pieces of legislation almost one hundred years after the United States ratified the Fifteenth Amendment in 1870, giving Black people the right to vote. Liberals needed change to make progress. The federal government was the primary source of that change.

Though Liberals appreciate the progress the federal government has made on our behalf, we still want to ensure we hold the government accountable. Just because liberal members of a party helped Black people get the rights that the Constitution protects does not mean they own our votes for life. They must still abide by rule #1—keep the economy growing.

MANY LIBERALS HAVE CONSERVATIVE VALUES

Some Americans believe that Liberals live their lives with liberal spending, low moral values, and even liberal disbursement of their earnings. I'm sure Republicans have helped along this thinking, since the Republican Party is now the party of Conservatives.

We should understand that we do not need to espouse the political ideology of Conservatives to practice conservative moral and religious values. I married my wife over forty-two years ago, as of the time of this writing. I've only married once. I have never cheated on my wife. Together we have birthed and raised six children. We took them to worship with us nearly every Sunday they lived in our house as minor children. We worshipped on Sundays even when we went on vacation. We still attend worship service on Sundays and Bible classes on Wednesday nights. I serve as a deacon in my congregation.

I'm a Liberal politically, and I have conservative religious values; I am conservative to the Bible, not some political party or ideology. I also believe that abortion is a sin. I believe that adultery and fornication are sins. I'm not sure that any of those things should be illegal though. I believe that the hearts of people determine their actions in their personal lives. The federal government cannot do much about them. I do not want a federal government that would do much about those issues. The values people exercise in their personal lives should be left to them. The Constitution makes that plain. My political ideology exists separately from my moral values.

In the meantime, these people, whether we agree with how they live their personal lives or not, are citizens of our country. They deserve our care and protection. They do not deserve to be hurt or killed because of the way they live their lives. We should not run after adulterers and kill them just because they do not live according to the Bible. Couples living together without the benefit of marriage should not be in danger of physical harm. Liberals believe that differences in moral values should not be a death sentence in America.

All my children attended college. We have three sons and three daughters. None of them have gone to prison. We all live lives practicing high moral values. That's not to say that we do not make mistakes.

My mom and dad were Liberals. My parents were married for sixty years before my mother died. Together, they raised fourteen children, all blessings from their union. By the way, my siblings are Liberals as well.

I wanted to display this picture of my life as a Liberal. My political ideology aligns with Liberals. I believe that the federal government can work for the people of America to accomplish big things that individual states, individual companies, and individual people cannot.

We should now understand that Liberals live lives that span a spectrum of moral values. Liberals who are also Christians understand, as

Jesus taught, that every life has value, regardless of their political or moral views. Just because I believe that a man who cheats on his wife shows low moral values does not give me the right to hurt him or strip him of his citizenship.

LIBERALS WORK AS CAPITALISTS

I started my software business over thirty years ago, shortly after the birth of our youngest children, twin girls. They became our fifth and sixth children.

As I mentioned before, my dad and his brothers had an auto repair business. They owned that business for over fifty years. The proceeds from that business supported our family of sixteen. Those proceeds put most of us through college. The business also employed several of my cousins and others outside of our family. Capitalism works for Liberals. Some Conservatives would have us believe that Liberals simply want handouts from the government. That is false.

CONSERVATIVES ATTACH NEGATIVE ATTRIBUTES TO LIBERALS

As the word "conservative" does not mean a person with conservative religious beliefs, the word "Liberal" does not mean a person with liberal religious beliefs. As much as people demonize Liberals as some sort of devils, we are not. Conservative politicians and pundits take the opportunity to attribute the lack of moral values to Liberals. It's an easy lie. Who would not believe them? Many Conservatives have few friends outside of their circle of Conservatives.

Voters have the same challenge understanding the meaning of the identity label "Liberal" as they do understanding the meaning of the identity label "Conservative." That's a real problem for Liberals.

That label does not mean we have liberal economic, religious, or moral values. Just like "Conservatives" gives room for allies to conflate other meanings, "Liberals" gives room for critics to conflate negative meanings.

LIBERAL PRESIDENTS SHINE AT RUNNING OUR GOVERNMENT

Liberal presidents have a great track record of running the government. Remember, based on the long-standing definition of liberalism, Liberals believe that government can play a positive role in our lives as citizens. We do not see the federal government as the problem as Conservatives like Jefferson Davis and Ronald Reagan do. We see the federal government as a partner in progress.

Importantly, for the government to have a positive effect on its citizens, it must run well. Liberals, during my time on this earth, have done the best job of using government resources to produce a positive effect for Americans.

The last three Liberals who served as president significantly cut the annual federal budget deficit by the time they left office. Democrats cut the deficit more than the last seven Republican administrations combined. That was not difficult. None of the previous seven Republican presidents ended their presidencies with smaller deficits—not one. Every Republican president during my lifetime claimed they would, but they all left larger deficits.

Bill Clinton campaigned for president on the promise that he would balance the federal budget. He won the 1992 election. During the same election, Democrats won control of the House of Representatives and the Senate. Clinton proceeded to implement his plan, with the support of both houses of Congress.

Clinton helped write, lobby for, and pass the Omnibus Budget Reconciliation Act of 1993, otherwise known as the Balanced Budget Act of 1993. It passed the House of Representatives without a single Republican vote. It passed the Senate under budget reconciliation, a special procedure that allows the Senate to pass a bill with a simple majority. Under normal rules, they need sixty votes to bring a bill to a final vote. A bill passed under budget reconciliation cannot contain policy that does not directly affect the federal budget. As in the House, the Balanced Budget Act passed in the Senate without a single Republican vote.

Imagine that. As much as modern Conservatives harp about reducing the federal budget deficit, not a single Republican joined the Democrats to pass the bill known as the "Balanced Budget Act." From 1993, when the bill passed, to the time Clinton left office, the annual federal budget deficit shrank every year. The annual federal budget moved from deficit to surplus in 1998. During the last three years of Clinton's eight-year presidency, the annual federal budget remained in surplus. He was the first—and only—president to take the federal budget from deficit to surplus since the 1920s.

Since the Great Depression, every Conservative elected as president raised the annual federal budget deficit by the time they left office. In fact, after Clinton left office in 2001, George W. Bush moved the annual federal budget from surplus back to deficit in one year. By the time Bush left office, he left behind what was, at the time, the largest budget deficit in American history. Though Conservatives *talk about* reducing the deficit, Liberals *actually* reduce it, even to the point of creating a surplus, as in the Clinton administration.

Liberals believe that the federal government has a capability unmatched by any other government entity. The federal government, with all its resources and authority, can bring the nation together and build big things. The Hoover Dam, the Tennessee Valley Authority hydroelectric project, and the interstate highway system are massive projects that no company could fund, build, and organize. But, more importantly to Black people, the federal government had and has the authority to move the nation past some of its racial problems. Courageous Liberals have led the way in doing just that.

We must always remember that, without a strong economy, our country cannot do much good. Good stewardship of our resources in good times and bad requires sound leadership and a tried-and-true economic model.

LIBERALS BELIEVE THE FEDERAL GOVERNMENT CAN HELP RIGHT MANY WRONGS IN SOCIETY

Liberals respect the federal government's capabilities and encourage it to keep doing big things. Bloody Sunday, as we call it, took place on the

Edmund Pettus Bridge between Selma, Alabama, and Montgomery, Alabama, the state capital. Marchers, led by James Bevel and Amelia Boynton, participated in a peaceful march to assert their right to vote in March 1965. The Fifteenth Amendment to the Constitution secured that right for Black people in 1870—but the state of Alabama did not respect that right.

Ever since the Fifteenth Amendment passed, the federal government never questioned our right as citizens to vote, but the state of Alabama had taken that right away—first with coercion, then with trickery, then with outright violence, and finally by changing the rules for voting altogether. By 1965, most Black citizens in Alabama, along with Black people in most other former CSA states, thought they might never receive just treatment concerning their right to register and vote, even though the Constitution guaranteed that right. But organizers of protests decided things would never change if they did nothing.

Once those protesters stiffened their backs and moved, the federal government backed them up. Once the federal government stepped in, the rest of the country noticed and supported their constitutional right against the heavy hand of their state.

In southern states, most of the domestic violence against Black citizens happened to deny them the right to vote. Medgar Evers, a civil rights leader in Mississippi, was mowed down by a member of the KKK. They did not kill him simply because he was a Black man. No, a member of the KKK shot Evers in the back in front of his own house because of his efforts to register Black people to vote.

Lyndon Johnson stepped up using the weight of the federal government and brought about change. Through a combination of his experience in the Senate and his power as president of the United States, he lobbied for the Voting Rights Act, ensured it passed, and signed it into law. John F. Kennedy had advocated for those laws, but he had died before he could get them passed and signed. Johnson grabbed the ball and ran with it after Kennedy's death.

Article VI of the Constitution states that federal laws "shall be the supreme Law of the Land; and the Judges in every State shall be bound thereby,"[i] Black people have always desired—and needed—progress and forward thinking over conservation and regression. When states stopped that progress, Liberals in the federal government stepped in and helped us.

In this case, members of former CSA states denied most Black citizens the right to vote. Liberals in the federal government championed that right and pushed through the legislation needed to secure it. The federal government succeeded in righting a pivotal wrong, in this case through landmark legislation.

LIBERALS DO NOT BELIEVE THAT THE CONSTITUTION IS INSPIRED SCRIPTURE

Thinking of the Constitution as a document inspired by God turns its authors into more than just regular people making an effort to organize a great government of the people. They were great men, but, like all of us, they were flawed men.

I like the description that Joe Pesci's character, Simon—a self-described homeless bum on the campus of Harvard University—gives in the film *With Honors*. Simon describes the Constitution using these words: "The genius of the Constitution is that it can always be changed. The genius of the Constitution is that it makes no permanent rule other than faith in the wisdom of ordinary people to govern themselves."[ii] The Framers had faith in ordinary people versus the belief that they were somehow inspired.

Truth be told, we all need progress. The moment we think that God created the Constitution, we make it something that the drafters did not intend. We also halt any efforts to make our country better when we need the Constitution to change to help it progress.

At the end of the Bible, God caused men to write that He would not allow changes to His word and that anyone who made changes would suffer dire consequences.[iii]

But the Constitution is not the Bible—far from it. The Framers of the Constitution dedicated an entire article to explain how to amend or change that man-made document.

Article V of the Constitution reads as follows:

> *The Congress, whenever two-thirds of both houses shall deem it necessary, shall propose amendments to this Constitution, or, on the application of the legislatures of two-thirds of the several states, shall call a convention for proposing amendments, which, in either case, shall be valid to all intents and purposes, as part of this Constitution, when ratified by the legislatures of three-fourths of the several states, or by conventions in three-fourths thereof, as the one or the other mode of ratification may be proposed by the Congress; provided that no amendment which may be made prior to the year one thousand eight hundred and eight shall in any manner affect the first and fourth clauses in the ninth section of the first article; and that no state, without its consent, shall be deprived of its equal suffrage in the Senate.*[iv]

Article V tells us exactly how to change the Constitution. It's not an easy process. After all, the wrong people could draft amendments for the wrong reasons and fundamentally change our government in the wrong ways if the process were too easy. However, the Constitution does provide a mechanism for change, for progress. After the Constitution's ratification by the states, the first ten amendments to the Constitution—otherwise known as the Bill of Rights—were written shortly after in 1789 and ratified by the states in 1791.

Men wrote the Constitution. These smart men understood that they did not know everything. They certainly did not know what the future held for this relatively new and different country, nor for its new form of government. They also lived in those times and knew that they left important issues under the table as they negotiated the Constitution. The drafters knew that we would need to address those issues going forward.

Two such issues were the international slave trade and slavery itself. In fact, about sixty years passed between the time the states ratified the Twelfth Amendment and the time they wrote, passed, and ratified the Thirteenth Amendment, which ended slavery. I started to write "only sixty years passed," but then I realized that sixty years equates to over two generations. Even a single additional generation of chattel slavery was a generation too many.

Liberals embrace progress. Progress requires change. Thank God the drafters of the Constitution understood that. So, when I think about the meaning of the identity label "Liberal," I think of progress—and I realize that progress requires change. The drafters of the Constitution, in limited wisdom, created a path for that change. Liberals have taken that model seriously. As they governed, they created and amended laws to enable progress. And, when necessary, they changed the Constitution itself to keep our country moving forward.

WHAT ABOUT THE REST OF US?

I have spent a fair amount of time talking about the reason Black people tend to identify politically as Liberals. After all, Liberals helped us when we were enslaved and could not get out of that situation entirely on our own. Liberals helped us when southern states stole our right to vote. Liberals helped us when we could not stay in hotels or eat at restaurants in many cities. But what about the rest of the country? What about non-Black Liberals? What's in this for them?

Good question!

First and foremost, Liberals respect the need for a competent, fair, and well-run government. Liberal presidential administrations have the best track record of fostering and sustaining growing economies. Liberals reduce budget deficits and run a tight ship with respect to using taxpayer money. The economy should always get first consideration in the minds of American citizens. Without it, we cannot do much. Without a growing economy, our federal government cannot accomplish great things.

Because Liberals value the power of the country working together to do big things, we know we all benefit when the federal government works well. The United States has about forty-eight thousand miles of interstate highway. Someone once told me I can drive from one end of the country to the other and hardly see a thing, but that's a different matter. The point is, I can drive my car from one end of the country to the other on roads built and maintained by our federal taxpayer dollars.

The federal government maintains awesome national parks. We can explore nature undisturbed by industry. We can watch the buffalo and other animals roam, graze, and live across more than 100,000 square miles of natural habitat. The federal government works with the states to make that happen.

And make no mistake, the federal government ensures that the states adhere to the Constitution to the benefit of all Americans. States cannot deprive American citizens of their constitutional rights and expect to get away with it forever.

Conservatives have made progress in diminishing the power of the federal government from time to time. A few times, this has been for the good of the country, but during my lifetime, most of their attempts to diminish the power of the federal government have instead worked to destroy our country. Some Conservatives agree with Grover Norquist that they, too, would like to see a federal government so small and weak that they could drown it in a bathtub. But we do not need that ideology to flourish.

I hope the last two chapters have helped you to understand the true meaning of the identity labels "Liberal" and "Conservative" as they relate to politics. We must be careful to use these terms correctly. We must not demonize Conservatives as being religiously rigid or Liberals as being religiously loose, because being a Conservative or being a Liberal says nothing about a person's religious or moral values.

We need to keep our focus on how each party runs the federal government. We need both those who respect the need for the federal government and those who want to make sure its power does not get out of control. We need two effective parties to make that happen. Sadly, the only effective party in running the federal government is the party of Liberals, the Democratic Party. That must change.

White Anxiety prevents that for now. We need to find solutions that move us past this point in our politics.

CHAPTER 4
HOW WHITE ANXIETY WORKS

> *When we whisper to one person lies against another, we can create anxiety. And that anxiety can play out in ways we might not imagine."*

WHAT IS ANXIETY?

Anxiety is a feeling. When a person feels anxious, they fear what they think might happen in the future.

ANXIETY FROM OUR OWN EXPERIENCES

Sometimes we experience anxiety based on our personal experiences. For example, if a dog bit me in the past, that experience might cause me to develop a fear of dogs. Couple that experience with my neighbor informing me that he has seen unleashed dogs in the neighborhood, and I might then fear walking in my own neighborhood because I developed a fear that a dog might bite me. That combination of incidents could trigger anxiety—that is, what I believe the future might hold for me if I walk in my neighborhood.

Anxiety based on my own experience is natural. I naturally use my past experiences to protect myself in the future. I can do this by considering situations that have caused me harm. Fearing that they may happen again, I do what I can to avoid those situations going forward.

We act based on anxiety, no matter how we developed the anxiety. I might not go out for walks in my neighborhood. I might carry a weapon to defend myself. I might call Animal Control to report neighbors who let their dogs roam freely in my neighborhood.

EXTERNALLY INDUCED ANXIETY

When someone or some organization influences our feelings of fear about the future in a way that has little or nothing to do with our own experiences, that can induce anxiety in us. The purveyors of this type of anxiety use it not only to control our feelings about the future but also to influence actions they want us to take in the future based on those feelings.

Some trigger our fear about people and situations we have not encountered or encounter very rarely. In their estimation, this will cause us to act to counter the possibility of the future they have groomed us to fear.

WHAT IS WHITE ANXIETY?

White Anxiety uses an externally induced anxiety to cause White Conservatives to develop an anxiety toward non-Whites and immigrants in America.

To create this anxiety, Conservatives use a very simple formula:

Predators + Prey + Grooming = Anxiety

First, I must mention that neither the predator nor the prey in this equation is real. The purveyor of induced anxiety makes them up. The predator/prey relationship only exists in the fantasy of the person or group wanting to induce anxiety.

Since anxiety is a feeling, the predator and prey never have to encounter each other to produce that feeling. In fact, the purveyor of White Anxiety hopes that they will not. In many cases, the predator does not actually exist—or at least, they may exist, but they are not actually a predator.

Republican political candidates use White Anxiety as a strategy to win elections. Instead of inviting voters to select Conservatives based on reasoned examination, politicians want White voters to believe that they are potential victims of unforeseen predators and other dangers. Repeated projection of fear, mostly about non-White citizens and immigrants, is intended to keep those voters on edge. This practice of repeating perceived threats is called grooming.

Messaging carried out by candidates and media outlets frequented by Conservatives fully indoctrinates voters, besieging them with fear. Republicans identify people of other races, immigrants, and poor people as threats. The White voter's fear, coupled with identified threats, causes them to self-identify as potential victims, the prey.

The next step requires Conservatives to associate those threats, in some way, shape, or form, with the Democratic Party, their opponent. Once the victims of White Anxiety believe that Democrats support their predators, Republicans step into the very important role of their saviors.

Since White Conservatives perceive themselves to be the prey of people supported by Liberals, Republicans now have the opportunity to step in and offer them protection. Republicans put themselves forward as the saviors of White Conservatives. And when White people begin to believe Republicans are their saviors, their qualifications, reputation, fitness for office, past political record, character, rap sheet, and any other decision-making criteria take a back seat to the voters' emotional attachment to Republican candidates. Republican candidates become their only choice, in fact. Because Republicans appear to be saviors, voters overlook their flaws. In other words, if Republicans are successful in this elaborate scheme, White Anxiety voters will only vote for Republicans.

The largest victim pool consists of American White people, but it can also include those who are adjacent. I would consider any American voters of other races who believe they benefit from whatever White people believe works for them to be White-adjacent voters. Also adjacent are those with an overblown sense of American entitlement, such that their feelings overwhelm their examination of candidates. We can also add to that voters who believe themselves to possess high moral values. They erroneously believe that this characteristic aligns them with the Republican Party.

And, as we found out in the 2024 election, White-adjacent people do not have to be citizens to fall into this anxiety. Many people of other ethnic groups, including documented Latinos who had not yet attained citizenship, rooted for White Anxiety candidates. After the election, several of those people mentioned that as ICE canceled their asylum claims and deported them or their relatives.[i]

No matter their opponents, those who successfully implement White Anxiety win elections. Unless their opponents expose White Anxiety or have a competing psychological approach that is equally as effective, White Anxiety candidates tend to win. Policy-oriented competition is no competition at all. Victims of White Anxiety only want saviors. Their condition has less to do with logic or policy than it does with emotion—mainly the emotion of fear.

HOW DO REPUBLICANS PRODUCE FEAR?

Key to the successful implementation of White Anxiety is fear. The Savior must ensure that his victims have sufficient fear of others. They must also see themselves as potential victims.

Remember the sequence: Predators + Prey + Grooming = Anxiety

The victims must not only be afraid but believe that if no savior helps them, they will eventually succumb to those who they perceive to be predators or threats. Under White Anxiety, the only winner is the savior. The savior promises protection from and eradication of the threat. The savior promises potential victims under White Anxiety that he will put them back in their proper place of control so that threats no longer have access to them.

Victims of White Anxiety end up with one simple problem: The threats that candidates have groomed them to fear are not real. The government can only eradicate real threats. It can pretend to eradicate fake threats, but sooner or later, their victims realize the threats were never real.

We've seen this happen again and again. Here are some threats from the past few years that have since been debunked:

- Mexico did not open its prisons and release millions of prisoners into the United States. The vast majority of those deported had no criminal record.
- The Democratic Republic of Congo, an African country, did not release people from jail and send them to the United States.[ii]
- Venezuela did not have low crime because they released prisoners and deposited them in the United States.[iii]
- Joe Biden did not open the border and invite dangerous criminals in.
- Somalians were not eating the cats and dogs of residents in Springfield, Ohio.[iv]
- Crime was not at an all-time high during the 2024 election.[v]
- Democrats do not like crime.[vi]

We should note that each time threats have involved people entering our country through foreign mass prison releases, the residents of those countries have been people of color. This has included Mexico, Yemen, the DRC, Somalia, and Venezuela. Donald Trump did not mistakenly follow this pattern. His goal was to create fear that people of color were invading America. These claims are all part of the grooming process.

But some potential victims might have no problem with people of color. To handle that issue, in all the fictitious cases Trump cites, he adds that these people of color are bent on their destruction. He says that their countries of origin released these specific people from prison and sent them to the United States.

All these threats seemed quite ridiculous during the 2024 election, but Republicans did not put them forward as rational arguments. Trump told lies about threats to groom potential White Anxiety victims. He contributed to the grooming process night after night in speech after speech.

Those victims did not know that Conservatives were grooming them. And, since most Democratic candidates had no understanding of White Anxiety as a complete strategy, they did not understand that these ridiculous threats were associated with their candidates. They filed the threats under overt racism or some other form of craziness. But, in the minds of White Anxiety purveyors, the equation made perfect sense:

Predators (Democrats) + Prey (White and White-adjacent voters) + Grooming (repeated lies about Democrats) = White Anxiety

Once Conservatives establish those elements in the minds of their victims, Republicans establish themselves as saviors from the predators. After purveyors finish their execution of this sequence, they have successfully induced White Anxiety. And during good economies, successful White Anxiety implementations nearly always result in a win.

WHY DO REPUBLICANS NEED WHITE ANXIETY TO WIN?

You may wonder why Republicans need to rely on White Anxiety to win. First, "It's the economy, stupid." As we discussed in chapter 1, Republican administrations do not lead to strong economies. When Republicans take office, the economy does poorly or tanks altogether. Every Republican administration since the Great Depression has brought about a recession.

In 2024, Joe Biden's last year in office, the economy created 1.5 million jobs. After Trump took office in 2025, the economy created 181 thousand jobs.[vii] In fact, at the end of his first term, Donald Trump became the first president since Herbert Hoover to suffer a net jobs loss over an entire presidential term. The economy had fewer jobs when Trump left office than it had when he entered office.

Trump couldn't run on the economic record from his first term. In fact, if he brought it up during a debate, his opponents would have crushed him with negative economic statistics.

Second, although wealthy people love to see Republicans take office because of tax cuts, middle-income people do not tend to see great benefits under Republican administrations. Republicans typically cannot point to a strong or even a good economic record of growth and prosperity. So, Republicans tend to use social issues and anxiety to mobilize voters.

Third, Republicans also need White Anxiety to win because they have great disdain for government. They tend not to make a great case for government in their campaigns. When Republicans promise that government will solve problems, they tend not to deliver. The ideology of Conservatives frowns on the federal government helping to solve any of their voters' problems that don't involve defense. After tax cuts and social issues, they have little left for which they can point to as accomplishments.

Fourth, when they cannot compete, they must delete. White Anxiety serves as a disqualification mechanism. Disqualifying an opponent is the electoral equivalent of having a case dismissed in court before it comes to trial. The Conservative candidate uses White Anxiety to disqualify his opponent rather than compete with him for votes.

So, instead of running on merit, White Anxiety candidates choose to run on fear. The promise of tax cuts funds their campaigns. They attract voters by acting as their saviors from all the people and things they have groomed their White Anxiety voters to fear. They will win if they successfully groom voters to fear voting for anyone outside of their nest of Conservatives.

SINCE FEAR WORKS SO WELL, HOW WOULD REPUBLICANS EVER LOSE?

The only thing more daunting than a perceived threat is an actual threat. Such actual threats—those that potential victims feel on Election Day—are more apparent than the perceived threats introduced by White Anxiety. Things that bring about personal financial jeopardy, the real threats, and their savior will win. Real threats might include the following:

- A bad economy/a dawning recession
- Economic disruption specific to the voter
- A stock market crash
- An ongoing bad war
- An ongoing or threatening catastrophe

Once the savior gains power and he or his party ruins the economy or causes some other catastrophe, he or his party may very well lose the next election. The potential White Anxiety victim's personal finances are directly threatened by a significant change in the economy. That threat is more real and immediate than the perceived threats introduced to create White Anxiety.

Another instance where White Anxiety tends not to work is in large population centers with younger voters. In most cases, these voters know people of multiple different ethnicities and races. They tend not to suspect that the people they know, work with, attended school with, and live near are predators. These White voters tend to see those grooming attempts by Republicans as poor attempts to induce fear of hardly credible threats.

When Republicans fail at running government, they lose. They fail to deliver on promises to their voters' pocketbooks. Winning an election with White Anxiety is one thing, but governing is another. Republicans can use fear to get people to vote, but fear does not work that well on other politicians. Also, the threats predicted during an election must be seen to materialize if their long-term strategy of fear mongering is to work. Somalis never started eating the dogs and cats of people in Springfield, Ohio. The belief that this ridiculous thing could be true served as part of the grooming process. But White Anxiety victims expected protection from millions of criminals released from prisons around the world and sent to the United States. They expected to see deportations of millions of criminals. That's hard to do when the total prison population of the United States is only 2 million. That said, the United States has the largest per capita prison population in the world.[viii] We can see just how hard a time a Republican administration, who sold these deportations as a rationale to elect them, would have delivering on this fantasy.

To answer the question directly, fantasy only works when everything else is going well. Once the economy tanks, fantasy no longer works. Reality becomes scarier than the perception of threats. Also, failing to deliver on promises to make life better causes White Anxiety voters to lose faith in their saviors. At some point, the government must work. The economy must grow. The leaders must lead with competence. When they do not, White Anxiety fails.

WHITE ANXIETY NEEDS ONLY A SMALL PORTION OF THE ELECTORATE

White Anxiety only needs to infect about 2 percent of the voting population to swing the results of the election. In 2024, 155 million Americans voted in the presidential election. White voters accounted for 124 million of those 155 million. Donald Trump won that election by a little over two million votes. Of 124 million White voters, Republicans needed only about 1.6 percent beyond the natural political divide to top up an electorate large enough to win the election. Successfully infecting two million voters with White Anxiety would ensure a win.

WHITE ANXIETY ALSO REQUIRES SOME BASIC BELIEFS

White voters must believe the following to be vulnerable to White Anxiety:

1. Our government operates best in the hands of White people.
2. White people are in a zero-sum game with Black people and other non-Whites—meaning any gain for non-White people must come at White people's expense.
3. Black people and immigrants are on a trajectory to win that game.
4. A specific politician and ideology can save them if they align with that politician and ideology.

Once White Anxiety exists in a voter, a politician can also convince that voter that he will save them from losing this fictitious zero-sum game.

WHITE ANXIETY REQUIRES DECEPTION

Imagine that the top 10 percent of income earners want most Americans to vote for their candidate, the candidate who would help their interests. The top 10 percent of income earners would not successfully elect a candidate who would do their bidding without resorting to deception to influence the votes of the remaining 90 percent. They need deception because what's good for the concentration of wealth is not usually good for most voters.

Imagine a campaign that says, "We want lower taxes, smaller government, less regulation, more favorable judges, and more government subsidies because those things will make our wealth grow faster. So vote for our candidate." That kind of campaign would not appeal to most lower- and middle-income voters. That candidate would lose.

Conservatives who run for office and share values and goals with the top 10 percent of income earners know that most voters will not embrace those business policies. Strictly pro-business candidates do not appeal to the average voter. So, those candidates must come up with a strategy that guarantees a certain number of voters will vote for their candidates, even at the expense of their own economic interests.

White Anxiety springs from that idea. Conservative politicians want most voters to choose a candidate without regard to competence or policy. They want Conservatives to make that choice using emotion, not logic.

If the bottom 90 percent chose candidates based on logic, they would never choose Conservatives. John F. Kennedy, a previous Democratic president, regularly repeated the saying "A rising tide lifts all boats." Based on the history of our economy, Democrats create that rising tide way more often than Republicans do.

The top 10 percent want to evoke two feelings in most voters:

1. Overwhelming positive emotion toward their candidate and their candidate's party.
2. Heightened negative emotion—even fear—against their candidate's opponent and that opponent's party.

Most Conservatives who run for office believe strongly that the federal government should be weak and powerless, except for its military. They rely on deception to attract voters. After all, as we look back on history, a weak federal government would have stunted progress for Black citizens. Some state governments run by White citizens harbored discriminatory feelings and participated in discriminatory practices toward Black citizens.

The legacy of racial prejudice lies dormant in some White people, especially people in and from southern states. That emotion stems, in many cases, from their ancestors having fought and died in the American Civil War from 1861 to 1865. After the Civil War, those ancestors opposed granting citizenship to former slaves. They taught their descendants that Black people were not human, and certainly not deserving of the rights that White people enjoyed. Some taught their descendants to justify chattel slavery, in which they traded enslaved Black people like livestock.

When the Fourteenth Amendment made Black people citizens, White people in southern states had no choice but to make Black people citizens. But some decided to make those former slaves second-class citizens.

Through a combination of terrorism by groups like the Ku Klux Klan and a coordinated economic denial of rights, White-run government and companies kept Black citizens from making much progress. Real estate agents, insurers, banks, state and local governments, and even federal programs propelled White citizens economically while constraining economic growth among Black citizens.

Many White citizens grew up during these times, but now most in the current population only know about them from what their elders taught them or from history books.

Many Conservatives work hard to awaken those latent emotions in modern White voters to encourage them to vote against the source of those negative emotions—anyone who would support Black people. In acting upon White Conservatives' negative emotions to choose candidates, they bring upon themselves (and the rest of us) a real problem.

We get saddled with candidates who believe that our federal government is hopeless. They believe the best approach to government is to dismantle it piece by piece. The people who hate government want to run government so they can make it weaker or destroy it.

Conservatives have successfully used White Anxiety on voters in southern states since the end of the Civil War. In fact, the transition of the Republican Party from a party of Liberals to a party almost exclusively composed of Conservatives accelerated when the federal government, led by Democrats, stepped in to fix racial discrimination problems in southern states.

Many Conservatives have never been happy with the federal government's intervention. But most Americans believed that the federal government did the right thing by restoring civil rights and voting rights to Black Americans after state governments of southern states illegally took them away. It causes white people to vote out of fear. When they do so, they vote against things that some of them otherwise believe in.

WHITE ANXIETY HAS A LONG HISTORY

Before Dwight D. Eisenhower won the 1952 presidential election, Americans had not elected a Republican president since the Great Depression began under Herbert Hoover. Six presidential election cycles in a row had yielded Democratic victories. After all, Hoover left office with unemployment over 25 percent. As mentioned previously, some Americans lived in tent cities called Hoovervilles and stood in long lines every day to get food. Hoover had no answer for them, only for large corporations. Hoover was a small-government conservative.

Conservatives do not really believe in using the government to fix problems for most citizens. Their track record bears that out. As the Great Depression worsened, Hoover had no government solutions for middle-income and poor citizens. After Hoover, Americans decided they'd had enough of Conservatives. They elected Liberals, and the Liberals turned things around.

Franklin D. Roosevelt, a Democrat, won the 1932 presidential election. Roosevelt created job programs across the economy. Roosevelt demonstrated that government could bring all those who were hurting back into the fold. He did not simply give them money; he got them involved in doing big things. With their hard work, they created massive and impressive things. They created monuments to American ingenuity and hard work.

For instance, the Works Progress Administration (WPA) hired 8.5 million American workers. The WPA employed thousands of Americans to build huge projects like the Tennessee Valley Authority hydroelectric dams, over six hundred airports, and over seventy-five thousand bridges. Roosevelt also created a number of other programs, including the National Recovery Administration (NRA), which employed millions of Americans.

When I worked with my dad in his shop, I remember he and my uncles talking about working WPA jobs. They mostly built roads in rural areas, if memory serves. But they expressed gratitude for Roosevelt's program. That program, along with many others, reduced unemployment and helped the country return to a strong economic footing. Those programs proved that the federal government could help during times of economic hardship, such as the Great Depression. A picture of Roosevelt hung in my father's business office.

After Roosevelt's success, Americans began to see the benefits of working together through the federal government to accomplish big things. Roosevelt's solutions ran counter to the ideology of Conservatives. But just as everyone, north and south, had suffered during the Great Depression, government programs had worked to lift everyone back up, if not out of it. And what programs had not done to completely restore the economy, World War II, when it happened, helped finish the job. By the end of World War II, the American economy had been completely restored.

WHEN TIMES ARE GOOD, WHITE ANXIETY MAKES A COMEBACK

It took a while—six presidential election cycles or twenty-four years—but Americans forgot what caused all that prosperity that lifted us out of the Great Depression. They forgot what caused the Great Depression. They forgot what set us on a course to sustained growth. They forgot what caused an expanding middle class for both Black and White citizens.

White Anxiety thrives during good times. Even though the policies of Conservatives tend to ruin the economy, cause recessions, and tighten liquidity, the farther we get from economic disaster, the easier it is for Conservatives to sow discord.

White Anxiety ceases to work during shrinking economic times. Liberals get elected during those times, regulate the banks, reduce the deficit, and ease the drag on businesses. Everything turns from recession to growth. Then things go smoothly again. And the moment they do, Conservatives conjure White Anxiety to make White voters suspicious of their neighbors and of immigrants.

Some might ask: Aren't Americans smart enough to see this pattern? Voters would recognize it more easily if the cycles were shorter. But three presidential terms are twelve years—half a generation. New young voters enter the electorate with no political memory. Older voters die, and their knowledge of history dies with them.

I'm writing this at age sixty-five. I've watched these cycles since Richard Nixon. When I'm gone, that knowledge goes with me—unless I write it down as I have here. This is an identifiable pattern, but until we expose it and talk openly about it, it will continue. And each time it comes back around, it gets worse.

WHITE ANXIETY IS NOT JUST WRONG; IT CAUSES LONG-LASTING DESTRUCTION

Lies are insidious. Lies always destroy something, if only the trust between two people. But they usually have a greater reach than that.

When we whisper to one person lies against another, we can create anxiety. That anxiety can play out in ways we might not imagine.

In the church, we have a saying: "Sin will keep us longer than we want to stay and cost us more than we want to pay." The same is true of lies. A lie holds us longer than we planned to stay, and it costs more than we ever thought we'd have to pay.

Lies eventually meet up with reality, the truth. And when they do, if we do not take the hit and admit that we have lied, we will tell more lies. That cycle will continue until we are forced to face it. A single lie will keep us lying longer than we ever thought it would, unless we dare to face the truth.

White Anxiety runs on lies. To plant fear in the minds of White Americans, politicians must lie to one group of Americans to pit them against another group. That's just wrong. Politicians and their advocates plant the seeds, the initial set of lies. Those lies grow into more lies. The level and severity of the lies keep rising with each new lie. That's the degenerative nature of falsehoods—things get worse.

The desire to live with integrity forces honest people to face the truth. But a real con man, a dedicated and professional liar, will never face the truth. He'll lie as the gavel comes down. He'll lie as the cell door closes. He'll take the lie to his grave. And each new lie costs him more of his soul.

As an electorate, we cannot rely on justice to fix fraudulent actors. Too many people have too much invested in White Anxiety to fix it through normal, moral means. Many will never come clean. The only fix is to stop falling victim to it and to make sure our neighbors and the next generation don't either.

At first, we are victims to liars. But at some point, we can become participants, passing on lies we've accepted as truth. When we recognize that, we face a decision: keep supporting the lie, or expose it, apologize, and move forward with the truth.

Supporting a lie requires no courage. After all, in the case of White Anxiety, we have plenty of company. Continuing to support lies that bring about anxiety allows us to move in the same direction as the tide. But when we decide we will side with the truth, life can get much more difficult. That requires integrity. And integrity always requires courage.

Liars will always find an excuse to keep telling lies until we get tired of trying to drag them to the truth. So, we must leave them in the wilderness of their dishonesty and move on. We must assume that they will never come clean. White Anxiety is only one of their tools of deception.

In his 1946 essay "In Front of Your Nose," George Orwell revealed this great truth:

> *The point is that we are all capable of believing things which we know to be untrue, and then, when we are finally proved wrong, impudently twisting the facts so as to show that we were right. Intellectually, it is possible to carry on this process for an indefinite time: the only check on it is that sooner or later a false belief bumps up against solid reality, usually on a battlefield."*

SUCCESS BASED ON LIES BEGETS MORE LYING

When the lies people tell lead to successful outcomes for them, the degenerative nature of lying takes over. If someone wins an election based on lies, they tend to run a dishonest administration. That might not be their plan, but it's just another wage of dishonesty. People tend to go back to the same till when they need more wages.

When a person becomes president of the United States, they become the leader of the free world. Everyone takes what they say with above-average credibility. If they have ever lied successfully—that is, if they have ever accomplished a significant goal based on lies—they become empowered by that success. And, once empowered, they tend to believe that continued success requires continued deception. That winning feeling emboldens them. That boldness in dishonesty has only one destination: destruction.

Lying always ends in destruction. Even if the liar is not destroyed, what he builds on his lies will eventually go up in flames. Whether he gets burned in those flames depends on many factors, but the destruction is present nonetheless.

White Anxiety is no different. Once a candidate wins through that deception, he can rarely escape it. The victory is real, but so is the burden—the candidate must now spend his time proving that his lies are the truth. That's an impossible task. Any candidate attempting it will eventually collapse under its weight.

JESUS SAYS THAT THE DEVIL IS THE FATHER OF LIES

In the book of John in the Bible, in the eighth chapter, some Pharisees use deception to challenge Jesus. They present a woman they claim to have caught in the act of adultery, and they ask how she should be punished. Think about what that means. Adultery is a private act. To catch someone in it, you had to be there. They were almost certainly involved.

According to the Law of Moses, when two people were found to have committed adultery, they were to be stoned until they died. *Both participants*, the man and the woman, were to be stoned, but in this case, they only presented the woman. If they caught her in the act, they saw the man.

But there is a twist. One of the accusers—a witness, according to the Law of Moses—had to commence the execution by throwing the first stone. So, one of the people who discovered her in the "very act" of sexual intercourse had to commence the stoning.

Jesus adds a caveat in this situation. A person cannot tell what is in the mind of another person unless that person reveals what's in their mind. People cannot read each other's minds. But Jesus knew the hearts of men. And, consequently, Jesus knew the truth about this situation.

Knowing what had happened, Jesus said to them: "He that is without sin among you, let him first cast a stone at her."[ix] The problem might have been that they were all guilty of adultery in this very situation; hence, they brought no man forward to face the consequences of adultery. Or, perhaps, they had all been guilty of the same thing at other times. One by one, they walked away—"beginning at the eldest even unto the last."[x]

He caught them in a deception—they were guilty as well. And to their credit, they didn't double down. This part of that passage tells us that they were all convicted by their own consciences, and they left one by one, "beginning at the eldest, even unto the last."[xi]

That is the best-case scenario of catching someone in a lie: Their conscience catches up with them. They realize they are wrong. They end the deception.

But that is not how John chapter 8 ends. Jesus gets into a back-and-forth with the Pharisees. They accuse Jesus of not being who he said he was, the Son of God. They accuse him of lying. Jesus tells them they are not living up to their lineage. They remind Jesus that they were Abraham's descendants. And Jesus tells them very directly that if they were Abraham's seed, they would do the works of Abraham. Jesus calls them children of the Devil. Jesus says:

> *Ye are of your father the devil, and the lusts of your father ye will do. He was a murderer from the beginning, and abode not in the truth, because there is no truth in him. When he speaketh a lie, he speaketh of his own: for he is a liar, and the father of it.*[xii]

By the end of the chapter, the Pharisees are going after Jesus to stone him. But that's how deception works. As someone becomes more deeply involved in deception, it becomes harder to get out. And at some point, they find themselves trying to discredit the person who forces them to face their deception.

That's how deceptive politicians work. They call themselves Conservatives, hoping that we will believe they have conservative moral values. Then they lie to us. If we are not paying attention, if we vote by emotion, then we are their prey.

Christians know that God hates lies. If a politician lived as a Christian, we would expect him not to lie. But being labeled a Conservative does not cause a politician to live by Christian values. Being a Conservative does not mean a person lives by moral values.

Jesus said a liar lives a life more on the side of the devil than on the side of God. White Anxiety relies on deception and lies. White Anxiety puts those who generate it on the opposite side of morality from those who live honest lives. If we act as children of the devil, we certainly are not living moral lives. And so I must reiterate: Being a Conservative does not mean that someone lives by Christian moral values. It does not mean that they live as Christians.

White Anxiety does not spring from high moral values. In fact, the goal of White Anxiety is to circumvent or get around sound moral values. Living with moral values takes thought and effort. Falling victim to White Anxiety means a person lays aside those values and votes with emotion. And fear is the chief emotion that politicians who practice White Anxiety want to summon from us.

CHAPTER 5
LET'S THINK WITH OUR HEADS

> *We cannot allow ourselves to be coerced, fooled, enraged, or made anxious enough to ignore the personal attributes of the candidates for whom we cast our ballots."*

HOW DO WE ELECT OFFICIALS? Do we not care about our country? Do we care about our economy? Do we really care who we choose to lead us? We act like we care when we make decisions based on information and history. We do not seem to care when we make decisions based on emotion.

I GREW UP WORKING ON CARS, NOT IN THE WOODS

I can now call myself a deer hunter. I did not grow up hunting. I grew up in Detroit working on cars in the automobile capitol of America. My childhood—and the childhoods of most of my friends—revolved around cars in some way, shape, or form. My neighbor next door worked for Cadillac. My neighbor across the street worked for Detroit Diesel-Allison. Other neighbors worked for General Motors, Ford, or Chrysler. Some worked in machine shops. My older brothers worked for Great Lakes Steel at one time. But in some way, most of our families, friends, and neighbors made a living with companies somehow connected with the auto industry. Even our aspirations involved the auto industry in some way.

In grade school, I remember a classmate named Lloyd who drew pictures in class. Lloyd drew innovative car styles. At first, most of them looked like some form of the Batmobile, but as I watched his progress through elementary and junior high, those styles became increasingly innovative.

Automobiles were all around us every day. We would see car carriers filled with new automobiles pass us on our way to school. And back then, we walked home for lunch and back to school for afternoon classes. When we did, we saw the new models of cars pass us as we walked down the main street of our neighborhood. We saw them on trucks before they were advertised or in dealerships. Rolls of steel from the Great Lakes Steel Works traveled past our school on heavily loaded trucks headed for the Ford plant a few miles away. We knew when model years changed because "changeover" meant our neighbors, in effect, got laid off for a month each year while auto plants retooled for the coming model year.

And because of our lifestyle, most of us grew up to work in the automotive industry. Lloyd became a designer for Ford. I attended a technical high school. My high school produced a boatload of engineers. I studied architecture. Many of my classmates became architects, and several of them designed the buildings that housed auto plants and offices around Detroit and around the world.

Our aspirations drove us to seek jobs above our parents' pay grade. Our parents wanted us to go to college so that we might fulfill those goals, and most of the children of autoworkers on my block in Detroit did so. In fact, most of the friends I grew up with have college degrees.

I grew up around cars. I did not grow up hunting.

LARGE BUCKS ARE HARD TO GET

My friend Franklin grew up in a farming community in rural America. We had vastly different experiences as children. He told me that he had never missed opening day of deer hunting rifle season. Franklin had hunted during every opening day since he was a teenager. In his community, many of his friends and neighbors farmed land. They raised, sold, and slaughtered animals. They marveled over farm equipment. And they hunted for food and recreation.

I have learned many things about deer hunting from Franklin since he invited me into the woods to hunt deer on his land. Franklin recruited a group of us unlikely hunters to his private land for fun and fellowship. Only a couple of us even owned hunting rifles back then. He also taught us a few things about deer.

Turns out that large bucks—older male deer—provide quite a challenge to hunters. First, large bucks did not get that large doing dumb stuff like exposing themselves to hunters. They became, at some point in their lives, skilled at surviving, eating, and traveling under the cover of the woods, mostly at night. They do not expose themselves to danger very often. They travel against the wind. That way, they can smell danger ahead of them. Deer have a keen sense of smell and can recognize the shape of humans and other predators. Humans carry a certain odor and shape.

Deer also have exceptional hearing. When they hear fabric rubbing against fabric or metal against metal, or they hear certain gait patterns, they can identify those patterns as humans. Deer can independently aim each ear in a different direction. That's amazing. Big bucks survive as long as they do because they move with cunning, ingenuity, and care. They use all their senses to remain safe by identifying and staying away from predators.

But every year, there comes a time when they lose their minds. That time of year is called the rut. During the rut, does—female deer—mate with bucks. Does interested in mating clear the ground of debris and urinate on the open ground, excreting a hormone that signals their readiness. Bucks smell that and find the does that left it. Bucks rub their antlers on the bark of trees so that does can track the path a given buck travels. At some point, a buck and a doe get close to each other. With the potential of mating at hand, the buck begins to be led by emotion rather than strategy.

They miss signs of danger that they would normally notice. Many deer get killed by automobiles during the rut because bucks chase does and one or both, under the emotion of mating, run into the road after throwing all caution to the wind.

For hunters, this is a good time to hunt because bucks are more likely to expose themselves during the rut. They enter open spaces during daylight that they would normally avoid. They put themselves in danger because they are led by emotion rather than using their keen survival skills. Experienced hunters understand this.

ARE WE LED BY OUR EMOTIONS?

Being led by emotion during the rut is natural. It's how deer were made to procreate. But voters are not deer and should be smart enough to be led by reason rather than emotion. Being led by emotion has made voters susceptible to White Anxiety. Being led by emotion hurts all of us when we fall victim to the emotions brought on by White Anxiety.

Unscrupulous politicians see voters as prey. During their normal lives, those voters act carefully. They consider their spending. They plan. They make solid decisions based on real evidence. Most people live responsibly and conduct themselves as reasonable people. They get along with their neighbors. They work well with other people and live good lives. They live by a moral code and expect others to do the same.

But during the campaign season, something happens. Unlike the rut of deer season, this phenomenon is wholly unnatural. Voters tend to split into two groups: Liberals and Conservatives. While the Liberals require competence, worthiness, experience, and some level of understanding of government from their candidates, some Conservatives seem to revert to searching for those who evoke some base level of emotion.

Those Conservatives, like bucks during rut, drop their guards when conservative politicians appeal to their fear of "the others." Suddenly, people they would not hire to do their lawns somehow qualify to run the government simply because they label themselves as saviors from "the others" at election time after inducing White Anxiety in voters.

When we hunt deer, as some may already know, we wear camouflage clothing. Deer do not have great vision. They know the shape and smell of a human body, but if we wear camouflage, they cannot distinguish our shapes against the forest backdrop. And if we position ourselves downwind rather than upwind, they have less chance of picking up our scent, unless the wind shifts.

Once we know what deer look for, we can make ourselves look and smell like that. But our intentions are very specific. We plan to kill and eat the deer. We dress and smell a certain way so that we might make them comfortable in our presence. When they look up, we look like the rest of the forest. If they cannot spot us, if we can hold still, they just keep doing what they normally do. By the time they hear the crack of a rifle, the bullet has already gone through them, severing both lungs and maybe piercing their heart. If we shoot in the right spot, they live a few minutes, or maybe only a few seconds, and then they die.

POLITICIANS WEAR CAMOUFLAGE

Conservative politicians tend to use the same strategy: camouflage. They look and act like concerned politicians. They seem to think that their policies will help us. The problem is their hubris. The problem is their confidence that their way is the best, in spite of all history and evidence to the contrary.

Many of these politicians craft a strategy with the specific goal of awakening fear and prejudice. They know that they can count on some Conservatives to react to that fear by, at best, voting for them, and at worst, staying home.

But because Conservatives will have sufficiently demonized Liberals through lies, distortion, and by creating "otherness," these politicians can count on their voters—especially those south of 36°30' north latitude—to never, ever vote for Democrats or any other Liberals, no matter what they may call themselves.

But key to the success of their "camo" campaigns is to address the issues that seem important in the economy. In that way, they seem to side with the deer, the voters. The voters suspect nothing. The politicians look like people who would help them. They speak in churches. They are against the right issues, the issues they have convinced their voters that any real Conservative should be against. They are in favor of the right issues, the ones they have convinced their voters that any real Conservative should advocate for. They have the right label, "Conservative," making them look like someone who would be careful with money and live a moral lifestyle.

Deer cannot see all the colors we can. Their vision is not all that good. But they have another ability that helps them survive: They can spot movement very well, especially human movement. Humans might be dressed as trees, but they do not move like trees. Deer can detect that. So, when a deer seems to be staring into our eyes, it cannot detect our eye movement. It suspects that something is not right, so it stares at us, waiting for us to move to prove what it suspects, but it's not sure.

When a deer tries to make sure that it is not in danger of being killed by a human, it stops and focuses. It can stay still and quiet for minutes at a time. The moment we move, it takes off, straight for the cover of the woods. Hunters have a hard time hitting a deer on the move.

As voters, we must have that same level of focus. On the surface, a politician can dress himself as a caring human being. He might act like he will govern our economy carefully. But keep staring at him. He might even present himself as someone who has compassion for suffering. Keep staring. He will eventually reveal his true self. Some politicians are so good at pretending that it takes time to detect the truth. But most of the time, we can spot phonies easily. We must keep paying attention, stay suspicious, and never dismiss any opponents as options until they count themselves out.

Think of the famous saying, "It ain't what you do not know that gets you in trouble. It's what you know for sure that just ain't so." Giving a party or a candidate unquestioned loyalty is not in our best interests, nor in the country's. It signals that we know for sure they will work best for the country. Many times, that "just ain't so."

Some businessmen will not do business with men who cheat on their wives. To them, if the person who sleeps in the bed next to a man cannot trust him, neither can a customer or partner—and a business deal with someone whom they cannot trust is not a good deal. Warren

Buffett, whom we discussed earlier, once said, "You can't make a good deal with a bad person."

Elections should cause us to heighten our senses, not dull them. During election time, we must move with heightened scrutiny. Who is the person we are considering voting for? What has he done in the past? Is he worthy of my trust? Does he have a résumé that says he can do the job? The best predictor of future behavior is past behavior.

Keep staring. Keep watching. The buck that gives up staring too soon, when he knows something is not quite right, ends up in the hunter's freezer.

ONCE IN OFFICE, THEY DO NOT CARE

In January 2026, the ACA subsidies expired. Many Republican voters who relied on those subsidies to help fund some portion of their health insurance premiums lost their coverage. Also, many Americans who did not take advantage of subsidies saw their health insurance premiums increase simply because the insurance pool shrank by millions, raising the cost per person left in the pool. Even businesses now pay higher premiums for their covered employees.

During the 2024 presidential campaign, Kamala Harris warned voters that Donald Trump would allow the ACA subsidies to expire and that millions of Americans of all stripes would lose their health insurance. She knew that because Trump had stripped critical funding for the ACA during his first term. Joe Biden restored parts of it, but to get additional funding passed by Republicans, he had to make that restoration temporary.

I remember when the ACA went into effect in 2014. I had two friends who both had small businesses. Neither had health insurance, but for two different reasons.

Jackson had diabetes. Having a chronic preexisting medical condition precluded him from purchasing health insurance. At the same time, he had a goiter around his neck that he needed removed. The removal would require surgery and a hospital stay. No doctor or hospital would remove the goiter unless Jackson had active health insurance. Neither the hospital nor the doctor wanted to take the risk of a complication during surgery that would land Jackson in intensive care, where his bill would escalate by thousands of dollars per day. Jackson could not purchase health insurance, so Jackson could not get his goiter removed.

Antonin, on the other hand, had no preexisting conditions. His business did not generate as much income as Jackson's, and he had no pressing need for health insurance. While Antonin was filling out his tax returns, his accountant told him that buying health insurance under the ACA would cost him less than the penalty he would incur if he did not buy it, so Antonin made the smart choice and bought insurance for himself and his family. He purchased the insurance on his local ACA exchange for less than $10 per month.

Jackson, upon purchasing his policy when the ACA became active, immediately had his goiter removed. He had no complications, and his goiter tested negative for cancer.

Antonin, on the other hand, experienced a massive heart attack that same year. Antonin spent over a week in intensive care. He survived the heart attack, regained his health, and went back to work. Without the insurance, who knows how the hospital would have treated him when he required intensive care for so long? And if they had treated him with the same care they did when the insurance company paid for his stay, the hospital would certainly have become less financially viable. Without insurance, that long stay would have bankrupted Antonin for sure. The hospital would have charged Antonin the tens of thousands of dollars his stay cost them. To avoid such bills overwhelming their financial lives, many Americans file for bankruptcy.

A few years later, Antonin's wife received a breast cancer diagnosis. Her cancer presented at stage three. Chemotherapy had to start immediately to increase the chances that she would beat the cancer and have a good prognosis going forward.

These are the stories of two real people whom I know personally. I am sure that there are millions of other stories like Jackson's and Antonin's. The ACA is not the best possible incarnation of federally subsidized health insurance, but it is the only comprehensive plan any party has presented to the American people in modern history that has passed into law.

Not many anticipated, when they voted during the 2024 election, that the outcome would cause such problems with our health insurance market. Many politicians convinced their voters that the reality that has now come to pass would never happen. Democrats warned everyone, but many who voted with emotion voted against their own interests.

Now that premiums have skyrocketed, those same White Anxiety–inducing politicians seek to gaslight those who voted for them. They blame the premium hikes on a flaw in the ACA itself. They try to convince their constituents that they will have a better plan soon.

The ideologies of these Conservatives preclude them from developing a government-run solution on the scale of the ACA. No matter how many lives their failure to support government-run health insurance costs, conservative ideology will win. Conservatives' ideology says the government should keep out of these types of services, even if Americans have no other alternative.

So, voting out of emotion for or against one politician or another can cost us dearly. We must make the ballot box a place of sober-minded, well-considered, evidence-based decision-making. The lives of many Americans depend on all of us making the right choice.

FDR FACED DOWN CONSERVATIVES

During Franklin D. Roosevelt's first reelection campaign in 1936, he faced Republican nominee Alf Landon. At that point, seven years had gone by since the beginning of the Great Depression. Roosevelt had thrown many federal programs at the problem. During his first four-year term, Roosevelt used those programs to shore up the banks, secure the elderly financially through Social Security, and cut the unemployment rate nearly in half. Instead of the supply-side strategies Hoover had used, Roosevelt had focused on the demand side, the workers. Roosevelt's programs and his continuing relationship with average citizens during that dark financial time in American history had made him very popular. Landon tried to dress himself in the camouflage of parts of that success.

Roosevelt gave a speech at the 1936 Democratic National Convention in which he mocked Landon and the Republicans as trying to steal the thunder of the programs that the Democratic Party had created. He spoke as if they were saying the following during their campaign:

> "*We believe in Social Security.*
> *We believe in work for the unemployed.*
> *We believe in saving homes.*
> *Cross our hearts and hope to die.*
> *We believe in all these things.*
> *But we do not like the way the present administration is doing them.*
> *Just turn them over to us.*
> *We will do all of them.*
> *We will do more of them.*
> *We will do them better.*
> *And most important of all, the doing of them will not cost anybody anything."*

Landon and the Republicans put on a disguise to win the election. More than likely, none of the things they promised to do—"cross [their] hearts and hope to die"—would have happened. More than likely, like Donald Trump in 2025, they would have cut or eliminated those programs. They would have plunged the economy into an even deeper depression. Fortunately for the American people, nothing worked on them. Racism did not work. Conservatives embracing popular programs created by Liberals did not work. The voters' immediate threat took precedence. FDR, with his campaign savvy, exposed the Republicans' camouflage campaign for what it was: subterfuge.

WE CAN NO LONGER MAKE DECISIONS BASED ON EMOTION

Camouflaged candidates who seek power should not attain power because they have the right labels and excite the right emotions. We are not deer in the forest trying to survive. Our hunters come after us in the open. These candidates make themselves available for questions. In most cases, we can research their public service records and reputations.

Picking a candidate to support is not as difficult as it might seem. If we decide to pick candidates based on merit, the process is easy. But we cannot do that if we allow candidates to appeal to our emotions rather than our good sense. That's what White Anxiety does.

We need at least two productive parties. Both parties must believe in government "of the people, by the people, for the people." And right now, too many people in the Republican Party think negatively of the federal government. They still subscribe to Ronald Reagan's philosophy about the federal government that we discussed earlier: "The nine most frightening words in the English language are 'I'm from the government, and I'm here to help.'"

In reality, if any of us were sitting on the roof of our house because our entire neighborhood is literally under water, and a person in a motorboat from the Federal Emergency Management Agency (FEMA) rode up and said, "I'm from FEMA [the government], and I'm here to help," we would be being dishonest if we said we would not appreciate their work and their words.

Yet when Conservatives attend rallies, they all laugh and agree that the federal government cannot do anything right, even though the government does many things right. Many Conservatives just go along with the crowd, knowing they drove to those rallies on interstate highways funded by the federal government in cars that met federal crash-test standards, braking requirements, airbag requirements, seat belt requirements, fuel-efficiency standards, and overall safety standards. They live in homes that meet the building codes set by governments. And some of them receive Social Security checks into their accounts or mailboxes on time every month. Others benefit from Medicare as their health insurer.

But for some reason, these people find it fashionable to claim that the government cannot do anything right. Obviously, it can and does. We do not have to lie to ourselves and others when we know the truth. Do not let appeals to your emotion cause you to make bad decisions.

HOW TO IDENTIFY A WHITE ANXIETY CANDIDATE

White Anxiety candidates want White people to vote for them out of fear of their opponents and their opponents' party. We can easily identify those candidates if we listen to their rhetoric with an educated ear.

Look for these attributes in a White Anxiety candidate:

- Talks about his opponent more than about himself.
- Attempts to evoke fear in White people concerning their opponent.
- Has few or no solutions to current problems.
- Assumes that White people find him credible based on his party affiliation, skin color, or both.
- Assumes that White people will vote for him because they could never vote for his opponent.
- Whispers derogatory or racist things about his opponent.

The whisper campaign is the worst part of White Anxiety campaigns. Many White people will not find racism or other -isms in national advertising. White people will experience those kinds of appeals in private settings. Sometimes those whispers will happen among friends or relatives. Many will experience those whispers on their social media feeds. But make no mistake, the whisper campaign is just as much a part of the campaign to win the allegiance of White people as any other part of the campaign.

Not every Conservative who runs for office practices White Anxiety. Some run because they genuinely believe they can make a difference—they want to implement fiscally responsible policy, small government, and the like. Those candidates come with detailed plans.

They focus on what they intend to do and how they intend to do it. If the bulk of a campaign is about that, don't lump it in with White Anxiety.

We should make sure that any candidate we vote for has plans. Ideologies are interesting, but they are not policy. People do not get health insurance from ideologies. The government creates new possibilities through well-thought-out policy. I remember when the ACA debate took place in the House and the Senate. Republicans held up stacks of paper and complained that the ACA bill had over one thousand pages of policy. "It was just too much," they said. Too much? How many pages should it take to fix America's health insurance crisis?

They were expressing an ideology. They did not want complex government programs. They wanted simple programs or no government programs at all. That sounds clean ideologically, but people with preexisting conditions could not get health insurance. And if those people qualified, insurance companies charged prices well beyond what they could afford. Americans needed a solution, not ideology.

People with preexisting conditions did not care how many pages the law contained. They trusted their representatives to vote in such a way that would secure what they needed: insurance. And they were willing to pay a fair price for it. The ACA provided access to that insurance. Ideology is interesting, but policy makes things happen.

When we ask candidates how they plan to solve real problems, their answers reveal everything. If the answer is mostly about the opposing party or the previous administration, that's a problem. Explaining who caused a problem is fine, but it should be a minor part of the answer. The solution is what distinguishes a White Anxiety candidate from one who actually plans to govern.

CANDIDATES SHOULD TELL US WHAT THEY HAVE TO OFFER

Imagine if I were interviewing for a job as a writer and the interviewer asked me, "How do you think you can help our company produce quality writing?"—but when I answered, instead of talking about my strengths as a writer, I talked about the weaknesses of all the other potential candidates. I majored in math, so I told the interviewer that English majors write worse than any other writers. I went on to say that philosophy majors are all over the place in their writing. And physics majors? Don't get me started! They write too theoretically. But *I'm* a good writer and therefore the best for the job.

Count the number of sentences spoken about the opponents. Then count the number of sentences spoken about the candidate. If the candidate tells voters substantially more about his opponent than himself, that's trouble. Explaining to voters how he would do the job is not his goal. Convincing voters of his competence is not his goal either. He is attempting to create a bond with voters around a common enemy or enemies. But we should want knowledge, understanding, and competence in a candidate. We do not need camaraderie around a common enemy.

THE GOVERNMENT IS NOT THE CHURCH, AND THE CHURCH IS NOT THE GOVERNMENT

Emotional connection is the stock-in-trade of Conservatives in modern American politics. Issues like abortion, selective sexual morality, racial prejudice, and immigration all have an emotional component. The things Conservatives railed against, in many cases, are not things the government can readily fix, but they are things that can heighten the emotions of voters and cause them to relate emotionally with candidates.

I'm a Christian, so I understand. I have a spiritual, emotional, and intellectual connection with the church. But the church is not the government of the United States, and the United States government is not the church. I want people to live better lives. I want people to live according to the teachings of Jesus Christ. But the government cannot make that happen. The church must work toward that.

I would rather our political leaders live lives that would qualify them as church leaders. To become a deacon in my congregation, I had to be the husband of one wife. I had to raise my children in subjection to our leadership in the home. According to the Bible, I could not have one child in my house and another child in another woman's household and still qualify as a deacon. I could not have cheated on my wife, dumped her for another woman, and then married that woman and still qualified to be a deacon.[i]

But the United States government is not the church, and the church is not the government. I would never allow a candidate for a government position to make an emotional connection with me because he said he was going to do something about husbands who cheat on their wives. That would not make sense. Nor would I make an emotional connection with a candidate who simply excoriated his opponent for cheating on his wife.

WHAT DOES A CANDIDATE PLAN TO DO ONCE ELECTED?

As a candidate interviews for my vote, I want to know what he has to offer and what he plans to do. I want to know what he believes about this country. I want to know his track record as a person. And I want to know what he advocates for. What I do not want to know—at least, not as much—is what he thinks about his opponent. Give me the facts and let me make the decision.

We need our government to do a few things well:

- Americans need to be safe. We do not need war. We need to be protected from our enemies through defense.
- Americans need a functioning economy. We need free and fair trade within our country. We also need fair trade with other countries.
- Americans need an honest government. We need officials who serve the interests of the American people and not themselves. We need people who will tell us the truth.
- Americans need a fair justice system. When we have disputes, we need clear adjudication of those disputes in a justice system that relies on the Constitution and our laws to make decisions. And when members of our society are accused of breaking the law, they should expect their fair day in court. We need politics out of our justice system.

- Americans need fair taxation. We understand that our government needs money from all its citizens to support the necessary work it does. Citizens' income should be taxed fairly. We need to get rid of the unfair taxation advantages for those who are very wealthy.

We need to leave religious matters to the church and have politicians focused on running our country in a way that works. Churches need to leave running our country to the elected officials. I do not want to hear political speeches when I go to worship God on Sunday—or any other day, for that matter.

We should ask campaigning politicians what they have to offer the country. We should judge them based on their policy prescriptions. But we should also notice how much time and emphasis they put on policy versus how much time and emotion they spend demonizing their opponents. That will help us understand whether they want to inspire anxiety about their opponent or hope about themselves.

We, as voters, have a responsibility to our fellow citizens to make informed choices when we vote. After all, the people whom we select will affect the government, for good or for bad. And, even if they sit around and do nothing after they take office, they will take resources from people who could have made a difference.

CANDIDATES SHOULD MEET MORAL STANDARDS

Electing candidates who have little or no moral constraint hurts the country more than almost anything else we can do. We should never even consider candidates who have track records of personal moral failings like lying, fraud, and cheating. Remember, the candidates we pick will represent us in the United States government. They will also represent us to the world. A president who does not keep his word to other countries can cost American lives.

We need candidates who earn their seats. They should have a track record of accomplishment. They should have a demeanor conducive to collegiality and honesty. Representatives who can negotiate and compromise accomplish more than representatives who hold a fixed position. We should not support candidates who simply follow the lead of their party over the needs of their constituents.

Polarization only takes one side. Negotiation takes two. If either of the two responsible parties refuses to negotiate, no negotiation can take place. When that happens, the country cannot move forward. It's just that delicate. It's just that simple.

For the life of me, I cannot understand what makes a stubborn leader attractive to voters. But, for some reason, we seem to have elected a whole crop of stubborn leaders. I call them leaders because they occupy positions of leadership, but they do not act as leaders. Voters elected them to represent their districts or their states. However, leaders have an array of tools in their toolboxes. They should always have negotiation and compromise in their tool sets.

BE SUSPICIOUS OF BUSINESSMEN

We belong to a country known for accomplishing big things and making great breakthroughs. We can only carry that legacy forward with able leadership. Somewhere, someone convinced us that people who have run businesses run government better than any other people. The businesspeople who have run the country in my lifetime have convinced me otherwise.

The two businessmen that I remember as presidents were George W. Bush and Donald Trump. We could include Jimmy Carter in that list, but he never touted his business credentials during his campaign. Carter was a nuclear engineer, a naval officer, and a former governor.

The things Bush and Trump have in common seemed unlikely based on what they said about their abilities during their campaigns. The idea of having a businessman to run the government was for him to run a tight ship. The books should be in order. The balance sheet should be respectable. Our debt should be under control. The head count of the government should be manageable. All audits should be clean.

In Bush's case, he came into office as the first president of the United States to have earned a master of business administration (MBA). Bush had headed a professional baseball team and served as governor of Texas. He was not just a businessman; he had served as the executive of a large state. In addition, he was of course the son of a former president of the United States, George H. W. Bush.

Bush Jr.'s résumé looked pretty good. On paper, he looked like a good fit. If being a businessman with a track record of managing a state did not qualify someone to be president, I'm not sure what would.

Bush's problems had more to do with his ideology and unwillingness to compromise than anything else. He seemed to believe that once he won the presidency and controlled both houses of Congress, his party could operate on its own. He did not feel like he needed to work with the other party.

George W. Bush took office with a $236 billion surplus. The news media projected that the country could pay off the national debt in less than twenty years. But Bush also entered office wanting to prove that the economics of Conservatives really could work. He wanted to prove that the ideology that his father called "voodoo economics" could work.

So, by June of his first year, Bush passed his first tax cut. By the end of that first year, the entire surplus had vanished. By the end of his presidency, Bush had left what was, at the time, the largest annual federal budget deficit in American history: $1.4 trillion. That was a nearly $1.6 trillion turnaround in eight years. It was an economic disaster. The unemployment rate had risen to 7.8 percent. The recession that started under Bush in December of 2007 was the worst recession since the Great Depression. Some economists called it the Great Recession.

As I said before, when the economics of Conservatives screws up our economy, Democrats get elected. Barack Obama won the election in the middle of the Great Recession. Whatever ideological accomplishments he had in mind had to take a back seat to the economic recovery the country needed. Obama, with Democrats controlling both the House and the Senate, turned the economy around. By the time Obama left office, the deficit had declined to $587 billion, and the unemployment rate had declined to 4.7 percent. Obama does not have an MBA.

The second businessman, Donald Trump, took office with that

$587 billion deficit and 4.7 percent unemployment rate. Trump had never held any government office before becoming president of the United States. Much of Trump's background was in real estate and reality TV, and he treated his first term like a reality show. He sent out government notifications on Twitter. He lied incessantly about big things and small things. Since he was surprised when he won his first term, he did not accomplish much until his second year. Trump cut corporate taxes by 40 percent. By the time he left office in 2021, unemployment was at 6.4 percent, and the deficit had hit another record at $2.7 trillion.

So, the theory that businessmen made better presidents has not worked well so far. Bush broke the deficit record. Trump then broke Bush's deficit record. The economy suffered a recession twice under Bush and once under Trump. Neither left an economy better than the one he took over when he entered office. Their predecessors, both career public servants, did much better jobs at running the economy.

The problem is not that Bush and Trump were businessmen; the problem is that neither was suited to run the country. Neither wanted to compromise. Neither had a plan that outweighed his disdain for the other party. Neither candidate cared about the economic well-being of the country ahead of his own supply-side economics ideology. Unfortunately, neither concerned himself with honesty and integrity.

As citizens, it is our job to discern these things. We cannot be so starstruck and rah-rah that our emotions lead us to vote for unqualified candidates. Spotting Trump's lack of qualifications should have been easy for us as voters. He never gave any detail about anything he planned to do. He made a good reality-show president. But we need serious people to run our country. Several people wrote books about him. The information about Trump was widely available.

Besides that, in his first term, Trump ran against the single most qualified person I have ever seen run for president, Hillary Clinton. If reading her name makes your skin crawl, White Anxiety has done its job. But we cannot vote based on emotion. We need the best person for the job. The job is too important.

Clinton served as a senator for two terms. She served as secretary of state. She was First Lady when her husband was president. Hillary knew all the world leaders on a first-name basis. She worked extremely hard and traveled more miles as secretary of state than anyone in that position in American history. And if we cannot vote for a woman to lead us versus a man who has been married three times and caught in a scandal saying he could sexually assault women, we should just turn in our citizen cards because we are not smart enough to vote.

Although running for president is a bit of a popularity contest, running the government is serious business. We must hold open the possibility that the candidate of our party might not be qualified to do the job. If he is not, a sober-minded, unemotional thing to do would be to not vote or to vote for the other party's candidate—we shouldn't vote for a candidate just because he belongs to our party if he isn't qualified. The office is too important for us to vote based on our emotions. Our country is too important to put into the hands of a person who could, in the best case, ruin the economy, and in the worst case, destroy our republic.

SO WHAT CAN I DO TO CHANGE THIS?

Look at candidates objectively. If peer pressure from our party or social circle makes that difficult, become an Independent. Don't identify with any party. Evaluate candidates based on their economic philosophy, personal track record, trustworthiness, and integrity. No one should feel compelled to vote for a womanizer because he belongs to their party. No one should feel compelled to vote for a liar because he has the Conservative identity label.

Listen to policy, not promises or attacks on opponents. If most of what a candidate tells us has to do with what he thinks about the other party or his opponent, beware! That's what candidates do when they have nothing to offer. They want to tell us who our enemy is. They want us to fear that enemy. They want us to know that our enemy is their enemy too.

In article I, the Constitution refers to federal offices as positions of "honor, trust, or profit under the United States." We cannot hand those positions to dishonest or untrustworthy people. When we do, we fail in our responsibility as citizens and put ourselves in danger. Those people speak for the country. But if their word means nothing to them, it will mean less to our allies and our enemies.

Part of the responsibility our country carries as a world power is trust. Our allies will not trust our judgment if those who represent us on the world stage have no honor. Our enemies might not want to trust what we say as a country if the leaders who represent us give mixed signals.

We need people who understand the gravity of their positions. We should exclude from public service and leadership anyone who believes their position allows them to do whatever they want. We should turn away candidates who operate in their own best interests. We should deny a place in our government to people who seek to divide and control us through White Anxiety.

The most powerful position in a republic is that of citizen. We must never forget that. No matter how much money a candidate spends, our consent—or denial of consent—at the ballot box is a power we hold. We can send the richest candidate, one who has the support of his party, including thousands of powerful donors and millions of voters, back home, denying him an office in our government by voting against him. And when we as citizens have spoken, there is nothing that candidate can do about it.

When we step into the voting booth to cast our vote, we must understand the power we hold. We cannot allow ourselves to be coerced, fooled, enraged, or made anxious enough to ignore the personal attributes of the candidates for whom we cast our ballots.

When we vote with our heads, we can accomplish so much.

CHAPTER 6
HOW WHITE ANXIETY THRIVES

> *So, it was not that difficult to turn White voters in former CSA states against those who supported restoring the rights of Black people."*

SIGNING THE CIVIL RIGHTS ACT ENRAGED CONSERVATIVES

On July 2, 1964, Lyndon Johnson signed the Civil Rights Act of 1964. That evening, he was reported to have said, "I think we just delivered the South to the Republican Party for a long time to come." Johnson had a unique insight—he grew up in Texas.

That very year, modern White Anxiety began as a political strategy with Barry Goldwater. Goldwater ran with William Miller against Johnson and Hubert Humphrey during the presidential election. The 1964 Civil Rights Act presented an opportunity to pit Whites in southern states against Johnson and Humphrey. After all, Johnson had lobbied for an expansive set of rights for Black people. The Civil Rights Act outlawed discrimination in hiring and voter registration as well as segregation in public accommodations. It removed many of the markings of second-class citizenship that southern White people had placed on Black citizens since the 1870s. The Civil Rights Act did not give

Black people any new rights. It just made denying Black people their constitutional rights illegal in statute.

Barry Goldwater ran on a core conservative platform of states' rights. The idea of states' rights seems innocent enough. After all, the Tenth Amendment of the Constitution guarantees states that the federal government will not capture any rights that states have not expressly ceded to the federal government.

But to people in states that seceded and joined the CSA just before the Civil War began, the phrase "states' rights" means something a bit deeper. They belong to families that have wrestled with the problems that sprang out of the defeat those southern states suffered during the Civil War. And though the problems that their White ancestors suffered because of the war were not the fault of Black people, Black people were definitely adjacent to that suffering.

So, it was not that difficult to turn White voters in former CSA states against those who supported restoring the rights of Black people. And since many Black people had begun to vote for Democratic candidates, Conservatives did not find it difficult to turn White people in southern states away from the Democratic Party and toward the Republican Party.

Some might wonder, "Why would southern White citizens turn against a party that enforced the rights that the Constitution had guaranteed to Black people almost one hundred years before?" All Americans should want every other American to enjoy the rights guaranteed by the Constitution.

In 1874 and the years after, a rash of election violence and intimidation riots deemed the Mississippi Plan had taken place in the South. Using that plan, White Conservatives in former CSA states terrorized Black citizens and prevented them for registering and voting. White citizens decided to strip Black citizens of their right to vote using violence. In some cases, they killed candidates who were Liberals. Between 1874 and 1964, Black people hardly voted in the southern states. It was just too dangerous. Because of domestic terrorism, by 1930, only 3 percent of Black citizens of Alabama voted.

If we do not know history or if we ignore it, White Anxiety almost makes no logical sense. It does make emotional sense and electoral sense, though. However, when we join history with a few other factors, we see that the emotions of White Conservatives caused them to move, even against their own best interests, to make sure the system Conservatives put in place a century before survived. Conservatives had designed that system to deny Black citizens of their right to vote.

SOME WHITE PEOPLE SEE A ZERO-SUM GAME WITH BLACK PEOPLE

Because Conservatives have influenced their thinking, White Americans in former CSA states think that Black people receiving equal rights—the rights the Constitution guarantees—creates a dilemma for White people. Those White people see any advancement that Black Americans receive as a setback for White people. They think that way because some White people see this racial relationship as a zero-sum game. In other words, they think that a plus for Black people becomes a minus for White people.

If I did not make the idea of a zero-sum game completely clear, let's look at a list of the components:

- It's a competition, a game.
- It assumes there are limited resources.
- In that game, gains minus setbacks equals zero.
- Only one competitor can win.

Right off the bat, we must see problems with this thinking.

First, Black people are not in a competition with White people. Black people and White people both deserve their rights as citizens.

Second, America is not a land of limited resources or opportunity. Black people and White people can both prosper at the same time. Gains by one do not cause setbacks for the other.

Third, since we do not have limited resources, retreats or losses are unnecessary. We can both advance and the game continues. Why? Because our relationship has never been a competition. Our relationship has never been a zero-sum game.

WE HAVE NEVER COMPETED

Black people did not compete with White people as slaves. Black people were treated as servants and had to do whatever they were asked. Black people did not compete with them under domestic terrorism. Black people were restricted from exercising rights guaranteed by the Constitution through local laws, lynchings, and other violence. We do not compete with White people now. We both work hard to advance ourselves and our families. We can do that side by side without anyone losing.

Now, we do participate in some inherently competitive activities. For instance, running for public office means competing with other candidates, and sometimes a White candidate runs against a Black candidate. If the Black candidate wins, the White candidate loses. That fits the definition of a zero-sum game for the candidates. But if the best candidate wins, we all win as citizens, and if the worst candidate wins, we all lose as citizens. That does not fit the definition of a zero-sum game.

We have so many situations that look zero-sum but are not. If we both attend a great school, we can both get great educations. That scenario does not fit the definition of a zero-sum game. But wait! What if a White person wanted the seat a Black person got and the Black person won it with better test scores? Doesn't that make it a zero-sum game? For that seat, perhaps, but not for education.

So, what would happen if the White person who wanted the seat was a legacy at the institution and thereby moved to the front of the line, bumping the Black student, even though the Black student had better grades and test scores and a better overall application? Doesn't that situation fit the definition of a zero-sum game?

I see several challenging scenarios that make sense. A legacy, in college admissions, is a person whose parents or other ancestors previously attended that institution. But think about this overriding idea: both of these people seek an education. They can both get an education and succeed. That means it is not zero-sum. They might not have seats next to each other. They might have to attend two separate institutions. But they both advance when they succeed at education. Neither had to retreat to allow the other to advance.

White people seeing their relationship with Black people as a zero-sum game leaves them open to White Anxiety. For instance, in modern times, politicians convinced some Whites that a Black man becoming president of the United States was bad for White people.

The problem that the authors of the Civil Rights Act hoped to solve involved securing the constitutional rights of Black American citizens. These laws did not grant Black people any special rights. The advocates for these laws wanted every American to have the same rights. They meant to address inequities, not in income or assets, but in basic constitutional rights, like the right to sleep in a hotel or eat at a restaurant. That is certainly not zero-sum.

Bad economies hurt Black people and White people alike. It does not matter which party or person brings on a bad economy. Bad economies cause people to lose their jobs. When they lose their jobs, marriages might break up. Some lose their homes, farms, and equipment. Others get evicted from apartments. The suicide rate goes up.

In 2025, as unemployment and prices rose, I saw advertisements claiming that immigrants drove up housing costs. I saw one post that declared that undocumented immigrants receiving medical care under the ACA would drive up the cost of medical insurance. From its inception, the ACA forbade noncitizens receiving healthcare under its program.

This constant pitting of "others" against White people causes anxiety and makes some White people believe that Conservatives—the ones who deal in that anxiety—are the only ones looking out for them, when in reality, Conservatives are the ones creating White Anxiety. They desperately want White people to look to them as saviors.

In the case of immigrants, purveyors of White Anxiety want White people to believe that immigrants caused the economic problems that tariffs actually caused in 2025. Then Republicans have a license to do whatever they will to anyone who looks to be an immigrant, even American citizens.

This is a classic scenario in sales:

1. The salesman looks for the pain points that cause suffering.
2. When he finds those pain points, he recommends his product as a cure.
3. If he does not find pain points, he creates them.
4. He convinces that person they have a problem that they just have not recognized yet.
5. If they have other problems, he turns those into problems his product can solve.

Purveyors of White Anxiety use all those techniques to diagnose someone with problems for which White Anxiety becomes the cure.

White Anxiety thrives when White voters believe they are under threat. White Anxiety thrives when White voters turn to Conservatives to eliminate those threats.

When White people work with Black people and others, White Anxiety fails.

Many of us have recognized that people somehow have an extra serving of guts and courage when they talk to us on the phone, but in person, they become much calmer and more even-tempered. We act differently with people we do not know, but when we get to know them—when we see them face to face, when we see them as our neighbors—we have a hard time treating them badly.

JESUS TAUGHT HIS FOLLOWERS TO LOVE THEIR NEIGHBORS

In the New Testament of the Bible, Jesus summed up the laws of the Old Testament, the laws that God had given to Moses, in two simple commandments:

1. Love the Lord with all your heart, soul, mind, and strength.
2. Love your neighbor as yourself.[i]

Of course, these two rules introduce an obvious question: Who is my neighbor?

In the New Testament of the Bible, Jesus faces that question very directly when discussing this issue with a learned Jewish lawyer.

The parable he touches on in his answer tells us everything we need to know about how we should treat people. It is the story that some call the parable of the Good Samaritan.

I do not like that title, "The Good Samaritan." It suggests to me that most Samaritans were bad, but this one was special—he was the "good" Samaritan. So, I prefer to call it "The Neighbor."

Samaritans and Jews did not like each other. In fact, some Jews despised Samaritans. Samaritans were people from tribes that followed their kings as their kings lead them astray, contrary to God's teachings. By the time Jesus came on the scene, Samaria, the Samaritans' region, was separate from Judea, the region that contains Jerusalem. The Temple, where Jews worshipped, was in Jerusalem, as commanded by God.

Samaritans were not welcome in Jerusalem, and they certainly were not welcome in the Temple. Jews discriminated against Samaritans. So, when Jesus tells this parable, the actors and their locations, nationalities, and professions are all important to the story. Jesus makes an important point to this Jewish lawyer.

The lawyer asks, "Who is my neighbor?"[ii] Jesus then tells the parable. When Jesus finishes the parable, the lawyer has no choice but to recognize that one of the people he probably despises is his neighbor. In the parable, the people who were obviously passing by the Jewish person in distress refused to help him. Robbers had left the Jewish man naked and half-dead.

In fact, when Jesus asks, "Which now of these three, thinketh thou, was neighbour unto him that fell among the thieves?" it seems like the lawyer, doesn't want to say "the Samaritan." Because he doesn't want to say anything good about any Samaritan, he says, "He that shewed mercy on him."[iii]

That whole conversation serves as a great example to all of us. It shows us that whoever we notice in front of us should be considered our neighbor. Their nationality does not matter. Their profession does not matter. Their income does not matter. Their political party does not matter. The only thing that matters is that they are another human being who needs all the same things we ourselves have need of.

In the case of the Jewish man who fell among thieves, he needed medical care and a place to heal. The Samaritan, without regard for his nationality, took this half-dead Jewish person and bound up his wounds, pouring wine and oil on them. The Samaritan removed him from the road, gave him transportation, and put him up in a hotel. The Samaritan man paid for the Jewish man's room, gave the front desk extra money, and authorized them to use his credit to pay for whatever the Jewish man needed going forward.

When we show brotherly love to one another, we operate as neighbors.

WHITE ANXIETY CANNOT SURVIVE BROTHERLY LOVE

White Anxiety cannot thrive when we come together. Once people encounter each other and start working together, outside agitation no longer works. Imagine someone in that hotel striking up a conversation in the lobby about Samaritans with the Jewish man the Samaritan saved from death after he regained his strength. The man might politely listen to the conversation, but I imagine he would not allow that conversation to influence him against any Samaritan anymore. After all, a Samaritan had saved his life.

That Samaritan had saved his life when he was robbed, stripped of his clothing, wounded, and left half-dead. The Samaritan saved him after a Jewish priest had passed him by and after a Jewish Levite had passed him by. I'm sure this Jewish man would see the world differently going forward.

Politicians cannot pit people against each other when people love each other. That characterization might seem strong, but it's true. When people see everyone as their neighbor, they never see anyone as "other."

My wife and I have three sons and three daughters. We love them. If someone came to me to tell me about how rotten they think any of my children are, they would not have an audience with me for very long. I would shut them down and send them out of my sight. My children are not perfect, but I know they are not rotten because I know them.

We should feel the same way when politicians try to pit us against each other. Many times, they use rivalries. They use sexism. They use socioeconomic differences. They use political party differences. They even use religious accusations. They use whatever they can to have us dismiss each other out of hand as "other."

When politicians do that, they have not earned our votes. Perhaps they *cannot* earn our votes based on their track records. Those tactics are cheap ways of causing us to vote for them based on emotion. Steer clear of that.

When we demand that politicians earn our votes, tactics like White Anxiety get thrown on the trash heap of history where they belong. White Anxiety cannot survive—let alone thrive—in an environment where voters demand sober, serious politicians who present real solutions. And if politicians who use strategies like that ask us to reelect them, they must show that they have accomplished something of note during their current tenure in office.

Most Christians have heard that parable of the so-called "Good Samaritan." The key to that parable, the catalyst for Jesus telling the story, was the lawyer's question, "Who is my neighbor?" We can imagine that the lawyer wanted to include some people and exclude others. He seemed to want confirmation from Jesus, who had also admonished his followers to love their enemies, that he did not have to include everyone as a neighbor.

Of all the people Jesus could have named as that lawyer's neighbor, he named the archenemies of Jews, the Samaritans. After hearing this parable, the lawyer could no longer exclude the Samaritans from the list of people he must count as his neighbors. He had to love them as himself, as Jesus taught.[iv]

I'm sure the lawyer struggled with that, but that is the place we must go if we are going to stop allowing politicians to control us with emotion. We cannot un-neighbor anyone. We must love everyone. Our love will keep us safe from tactics like White Anxiety.

CHAPTER 7
CONSERVATIVES AND WHITE ANXIETY'S HISTORY

> *Whites continued violently capturing cities and states using the same smash-and-grab strategy on Election Days. They carried out violent Election Days in every former Confederate state."*

THE FREEING OF ALL SLAVES CAUSED A PROBLEM FOR CONSERVATIVES

IN THE 1860S, Mississippi was the most affluent state in the country. Enslaved people comprised 55 percent of its population—the second-highest percentage after only South Carolina.[i] After the war ended and the Thirteenth, Fourteenth, and Fifteenth Amendments were ratified, freed Black people still made up 55 to 59 percent of Mississippi's total population.

In 1870, Black people in the United States had their right to vote affirmed. As American citizens, they already had the right to vote, but Conservatives challenged it in every way they could, forcing Congress to pass and the states to ratify the Fifteenth Amendment to settle the matter.

After having that right reaffirmed, Black citizens voted in large numbers for Republican candidates. Their votes gave Republicans—the party of Liberals at the time—control of the state house in Mississippi. Mississippi elected a Republican governor, James L. Alcorn. Mississippi also voted for Ulysses S. Grant, one of Abraham Lincoln's former generals, in the 1872 presidential election.

Black citizens voted for Black state and federal legislators. Because Black citizens voted at rates as high as 97 percent, they elected Black candidates up and down the ballot in local, state, and federal elections. Given Mississippi's population, the prospects for Democrats—at the time, the party of Conservatives—turned sour. They did not have the numbers to win. How would they ever win again? Nearly a decade after the end of the Civil War, and just a few years after the Fifteenth Amendment's ratification, Liberals controlled many of the governments of former CSA states, with Black Liberals working and governing fairly.

THE VICKSBURG MASSACRE

Politicians used White Anxiety to stir up anger in White Conservatives in former CSA states. As White Anxiety brewed in the hearts of those Conservatives, they devised a plan to take over the city of Vicksburg, Mississippi. They did not strategize politically or attempt to sell themselves as better stewards of the town's resources. They planned to seize control of Vicksburg's government by force during the next election. They planned a violent Election Day smash-and-grab to take back power from the Liberals.

They formed militias in the run-up to the 1874 elections in Vicksburg.[ii] They withheld weapons and ammunition from those who would help Liberals over the preceding months. Finally, on Election Day, those White militias used violence to prevent Black citizens from voting. White people killed some Republican candidates and physically prevented voters who were Liberals from voting for other Republican candidates. Under violence, intimidation, and murder, White Conservatives took control of Vicksburg. As many as three hundred Black citizens were killed during the riots that continued even after the election. This event gained popularity in the southern states as the Vicksburg Massacre.

THE MISSISSIPPI PLAN

Mississippi Democrats used the same smash-and-grab tactic throughout the state on Election Day. They denied Black citizens and other Liberals who would vote for Republicans their right to vote using violent gangs like the Red Shirts. That new domestic terror tactic of stealing elections through murder and other violence by White people against Black people on Election Day became known as the Mississippi Plan.

As the plan gained success throughout Mississippi, it became a model for other former CSA states. Mississippi and the rest of the former Confederate states voted for Democrats until the modern Republican Party emerged. The threat of violence became part of the culture. Violence deterred Black citizens from challenging their inability to vote in any significant numbers for nearly ninety years. Though Black citizens had gained their freedom and citizenship, the violence of Conservatives prevented them from having a say in their government through voting.

White Conservatives carried out violent Election Days in every former CSA state. White Anxiety encouraged White citizens to take up arms and fight against Black citizens exercising their constitutional right to vote.

These are some of the massacres that Conservatives used to take back governments after they lost elections to Liberals:[iii]

- The Vicksburg Massacre of 1874 in Vicksburg, Mississippi:
- The Clinton Massacre of 1875 in Clinton, Mississippi
- The Eufaula Election Massacre of 1874 in Eufaula, Alabama[iv]
- The Laurens County Massacre of 1870 in Laurens County, South Carolina
- The Hamburg Massacre of 1876 in Aiken, South Carolina

- The Asheville Election Riot of 1868 in Asheville, North Carolina
- The Camilla Massacre of 1868 in Albany, Georgia
- The Danville Riot of 1883 in Danville, Virginia
- The Texas Election Outrage of 1886 in Washington County, Texas
- The Forrest City Riot of 1888 in Forrest City, Arkansas
- The Rogersville Riot of 1867 in Rogersville, Tennessee
- The Colfax Massacre of 1873 in Colfax, Louisiana
- The Wilmington Racial Massacre of 1898, in Wilmington, North Carolina
- The Phoenix Election Riot of 1898, in Greenwood County, South Carolina
- The Ocoee Massacre of 1920, in Ocoee, Florida

All these massacres occurred for the same reasons. Black Liberals registered to vote and helped Liberals win elections, while Conservatives did not want to cede control of government to Black people or the Liberals they supported. Southern states used a combination of violence and legal restrictions to keep Black people from voting.

THE SECOND MISSISSIPPI PLAN

After White Conservatives regained control of the state legislature of Mississippi, they devised a plan to ignore the Fourteenth and Fifteenth Amendments of the Constitution in a way that they believed the federal government could not stop. They did so in their 1890 constitutional convention by passing new voter eligibility requirements in the Mississippi constitution. These amendments focused on defining criteria that made voter registration eligibility more difficult for Black citizens to meet than for White citizens, though it did not technically discriminate. For instance, the new laws contained a "grandfather clause." This clause granted voting rights to anyone whose grandfather had legally voted. No freed slave had a grandfather who had legally voted.

The second Mississippi Plan became a model for former

Confederate states. Seven other states adopted similar voter suppression laws. In 1898, the U.S. Supreme Court in *Williams v. Mississippi* upheld these voter suppression laws as constitutional in a unanimous decision.[v]

Violent election days, along with voter suppression laws, allowed Conservatives to maintain power across former Confederate states. Until the Voting Rights Act of 1965, only a small percentage of eligible Black citizens were allowed to register and vote. The power of White Anxiety not only allowed White Conservatives to take control of those states starting in the 1870s, but it also enabled them to maintain control, unchallenged, for over ninety years.

BARRY GOLDWATER DISCOVERED THE SOUTH IN 1964

From the mid-1870s until the 1960s, Democratic Conservatives maintained control of the governments of former Confederate states. In the 1964 presidential election, Barry Goldwater campaigned as a constitutional conservative and exposed Democrats' vulnerability in the South.[vi] He opposed the Supreme Court's decision in Brown v. Board of Education of Topeka, Kansas.[vii] He also opposed the Civil Rights Act of 1964. Goldwater became popular in the South because he said the federal government had no right to impose desegregation on any state. Mississippi and other former Confederate states embraced this idea.

Lyndon Johnson honored John F. Kennedy after his assassination by passing the landmark legislation for which Kennedy had advocated before he lost his life. So, Johnson used his nearly twenty-five years of legislative experience and his presidential power to push through the Civil Rights Act of 1964 and the Voting Rights Act of 1965.

The White citizens of former Confederate states had voted almost religiously for Democrats before 1964. The Democratic Party enjoyed the support of most Conservatives, but when Johnson supported the Civil Rights Act and signed it into law, that allegiance crumbled. All the violence of all those massacres across the South, the changes to their constitutions, and the laws they put in place to maintain power would come to naught if the federal government enforced the right of Black people to operate as regular citizens in southern states.

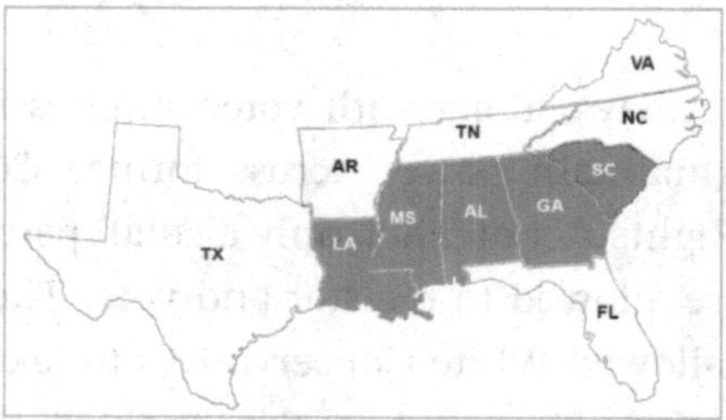

Figure 4: Southern states Goldwater won in 1964

Goldwater, Johnson's opponent in the 1964 presidential election, won Louisiana, Mississippi, Alabama, Georgia, and South Carolina. CSA states voted for a Republican for the first time since Black citizens from those states, who comprised a majority of voters back then, voted for Ulysses S. Grant in the 1872 presidential election. Goldwater's campaign worked very hard to win the South. In the process, he lost every other state except his home state of Arizona.

Goldwater discovered that Republicans could win southern states with the right message. Since the Vicksburg Massacre, the ideology of inflicting violence against Black people who tried to vote, along with voter suppression laws, had kept Conservatives in control. Goldwater argued in his book *The Conscience of a Conservative* that the federal government had no right to impose integration on any state. He also argued later that the Voting Rights Act of 1965 was unconstitutional. He believed states had the right to regulate voting.

Goldwater had that part right. States do have the right to regulate voting. The Constitution guarantees that right in its Article I. Also, the Tenth Amendment protects their rights as states, but southern states violated a different right in the Constitution. Honesty should have dictated that Goldwater exhibit the same constitutional diligence in stopping those states from looting the rights of Black voters using violence. Preventing Black voters from registering and voting directly violates the Fifteenth Amendment. Congress passed the Voting Rights Act to address that violation.

Goldwater exposed a path for the Republican Party. Southern states would align with any party that opposed the progress of Black people. Fighting the constitutionality of laws that helped Black people to register and vote spurred the emotions of White people in southern states. These people had vowed never to vote for candidates who belonged to the party of Abraham Lincoln. But Goldwater's promise to get rid of the Civil Rights Act that had been passed in that very same year proved enough for them to switch parties and vote for him. If it took states' rights to win the hearts of voters in southern states, Republicans happily exploited that route to the hearts of southern White Conservatives.

Goldwater's success helped former CSA states move from the Democratic Party to the Republican Party. This was the largest move in that direction since the "Lilly-white Movement" in the Republican Party attempted to attract White members and shun Black members in the late 1800s.[viii] Goldwater and subsequent Republican presidential candidates gave credibility to the power that Conservatives won and maintained in southern states through White Anxiety and violence. Over the next half-century, southern states would firmly align with the Republican camp, becoming states Republican candidates could rely on to vote for them.

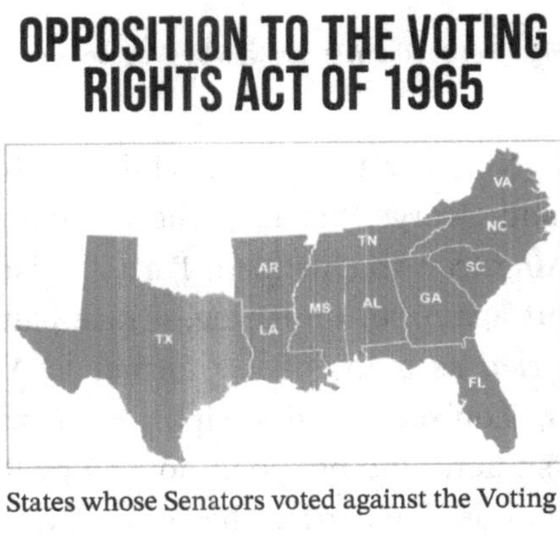

Figure 5: States whose Senators voted against the Voting Rights Act

If the Civil Rights Act of 1964 sparked former CSA states' discontent with the Democratic Party, the Voting Rights Act sealed it. Almost one hundred years had passed since the first smash-and-grab violent Election Days in CSA states.

As previously discussed, Lyndon Johnson introduced the Voting Rights Act of 1965 ten days after the Bloody Sunday march from Selma to Montgomery in Alabama. The U.S. Senate introduced the legislation with Democratic and Republican support on March 17, 1965.

However, Confederate states' senators voted against the Voting Rights Act. One senator in Texas was the only exception. The senators may have felt that all the Election Day massacres that their forefathers had carried out had seemed to come to naught. The former Confederate states have since kept up a steady stream of lawsuits contesting various parts of the Voting Rights Act.

GEORGE WALLACE WAS A NATURAL TO WIN IN 1968

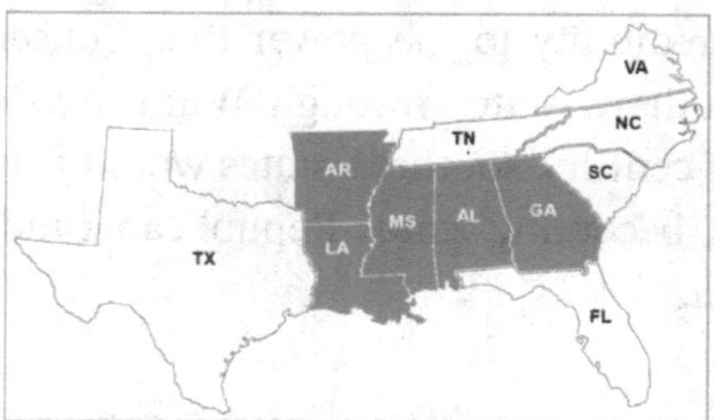

Figure 6: Southern states won by Wallace, 1968

In 1968, Richard Nixon ran against Hubert Humphrey of the Democratic Party and George Wallace, who left the Democratic Party to run under the American Independent Party.[ix] Nixon won the presidential election, but again, an underdog, a race-baiting Conservative from Alabama, carried as many of the former CSA states as Nixon, winning Arkansas, Louisiana, Mississippi, Alabama, and Georgia. Wallace's accomplishments did not go unnoticed by Republicans. For a second election, an underdog carried the South. This time it was as an independent. But importantly, it was not a Democrat. Wallace was also a Conservative.

NIXON WON THE SOUTH DURING HIS REELECTION

Richard Nixon ran for reelection in 1972 and won against George McGovern. The Conservative George Wallace also ran in the Democratic primaries this time; however, he was shot in May 1972 in an assassination attempt and paralyzed from the waist down. George Wallace left the race in July 1972. It seems that all the states that voted for Wallace in the 1968 presidential election went to Nixon in 1972.

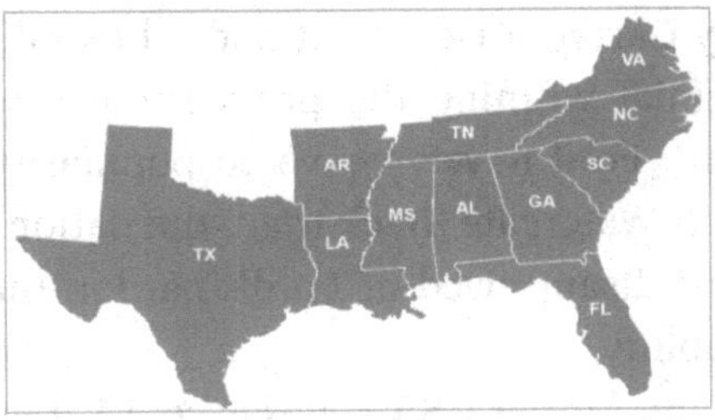

Figure 7: Southern states won by Nixon, 1972

This time, Nixon swept the country. The only places McGovern won were Massachusetts and Washington, DC. Nixon won 520 electoral votes. George McGovern won seventeen.

Nixon's campaign bugged the offices of the National Democratic Committee at the Watergate Hotel in Washington, DC. Before Nixon resigned for his involvement in the Watergate scandal, his vice president, Spiro Agnew, resigned his own position over bribery charges. Those bribes dated back to his time as the governor of Maryland and his time as the executive of Baltimore County. Agnew accepted bribes in exchange for construction contracts. Those bribes continued to be paid even after he became vice president.[x]

After Agnew resigned, Nixon appointed Gerald R. Ford as his new vice president. With Ford in place, Nixon resigned from the presidency. Gerald Ford pardoned Nixon on September 8, 1974.

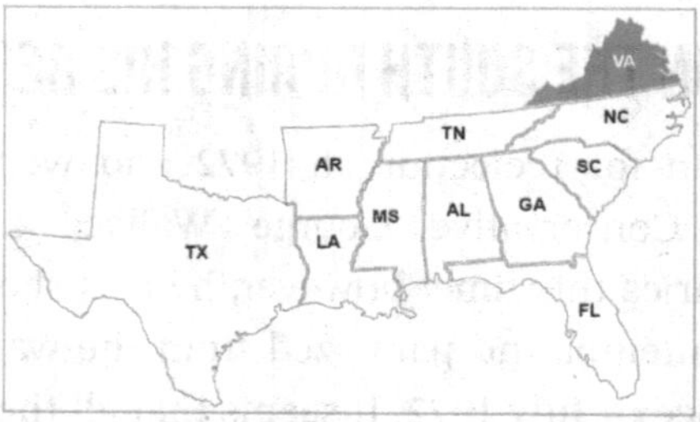

Figure 8: Southern states won by Jimmy Carter, 1976

In 1976, Jimmy Carter, a Democrat and a Liberal, won all the CSA states except Virginia, winning the presidential election. Carter ran against Gerald Ford. Ford never recovered popularity after pardoning Nixon for his role in Watergate. Back then, the nation cared that Nixon broke the law. Most disapproved of Ford's pardon that allowed Nixon to escape accountability.

Carter won all the former CSA states except Virginia. Carter ran as a Liberal. But back then, the default party in the South was still the Democratic Party. Carter would be the last Democrat to win a majority of former CSA states, even as of this writing.

Republicans realized they could win the South based on what Barry Goldwater and George Wallace had accomplished. Because Lyndon Johnson had passed legislation favorable to Black citizens, the South decided to move out of the Democratic Party's camp. Republicans developed a strategy. That strategy had to assure citizens of southern states that the Republican Party aligned with their desire to maintain states' rights. States' rights became a dog whistle for those who opposed legislation that favored the progress of Black people. But Conservatives argued that the federal government had no right to stick its nose into the affairs of their states.

In some ways, the cat was out of the bag though. The combination of the Civil Rights Act and the Voting Rights Act had started the process of racial equality, in law anyway. No matter what they tried, there wasn't much they could do about it. Going backward on the newfound freedoms of desegregation and voting rights never happened. In fact, violence associated with the deaths of Black people who tried to exercise their rights was now being prosecuted.

But the Republican Party had gained the allegiance of many southern White voters. Though they could not repeal the laws that Lyndon Johnson had ushered into existence, Republicans did gain their hearts and minds. They revived the hopes of southern citizens through speeches and coded language.

Since then, we can point to an obvious southern strategy during the campaigns of every subsequent Republican president.

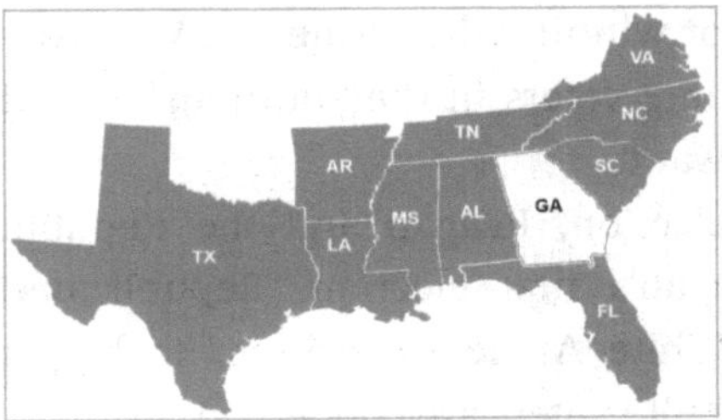

Figure 9: Reagan won the South in 1980

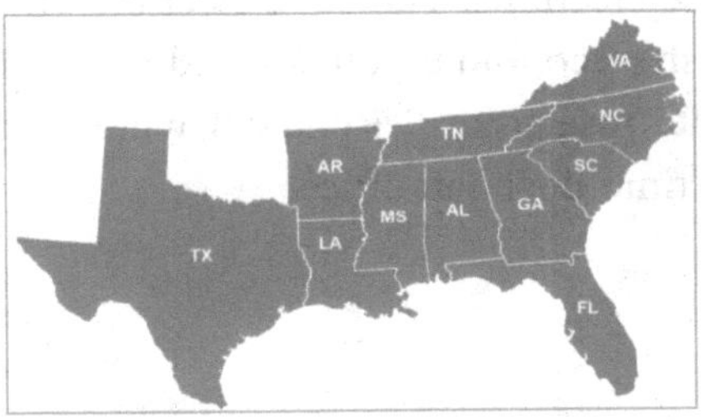

Figure 10: Reagan swept the South in 1980

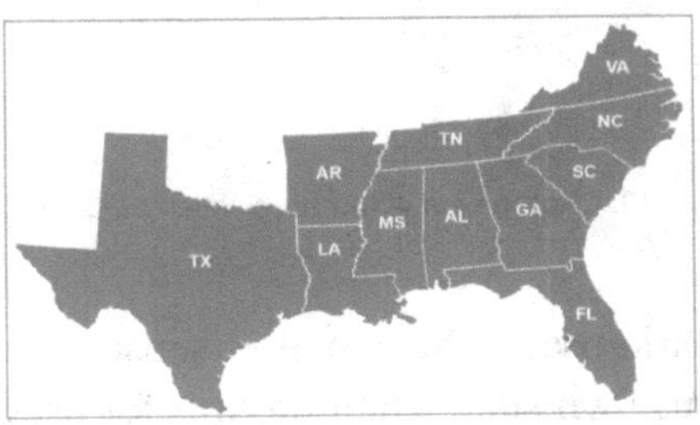

Figure 11: Bush, Sr. swept the South in 1988

After Ronald Reagan won the Republican nomination, he gave his first major speech in Philadelphia, Mississippi. He gave that speech at the Neshoba County Fair on August 3, 1980. Philadelphia was the city where James Chaney, Andrew Goodman, and Michael Schwerner were kidnapped and killed in 1964 during Freedom Summer.[xi] Chaney, Goodman, and Schwerner had been involved in registering Black citizens to vote throughout Mississippi. Reagan's speech gained him strong support in the former CSA states. His speech focused on states' rights, and it worked. Reagan won all the southern states but Georgia.

The formula for winning the former CSA states was set: Tug at the heartstrings of White voters in the South and promise them they can do anything they want.

By the next election, Reagan and the Republicans swept those states. Since Reagan's first election, Republicans have won most southern states. White Anxiety continues to help them stay on top where Southern White voters are concerned.

As I mentioned before, recessions and bad overall economies cause Republicans to lose elections. The 1992 election was such an election. George H. W. Bush's economic policies had sparked a recession. The unemployment rate rose from 5.5 percent when Reagan left office to 7.5 percent by the time Bush left office.

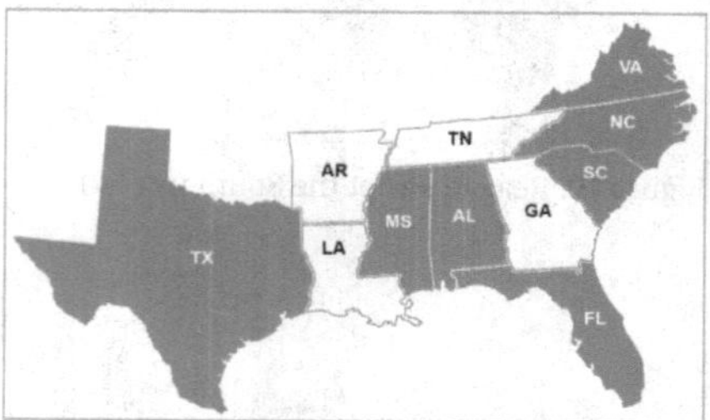

Figure 12: Clinton won 4 Southern states 1992 and 1996

Clinton won Arkansas, which makes sense — the governor of a state should win his own state when he runs for president. Altogether, Clinton won four of the former CSA states. The power of White Anxiety, even during a fairly deep recession, gave Bush wins in Texas, Mississippi, Alabama, North Carolina, South Carolina, Florida, and Virginia.

After Clinton won a minority of former CSA states in each of his two elections, the die seemed cast. The South, by and large, belonged to Republicans if they kept up their White Anxiety tactics. Clinton's wins seemed somewhat impressive, but he only won four out of the eleven former CSA states. A Democrat has not won most of those states since Jimmy Carter in 1976.

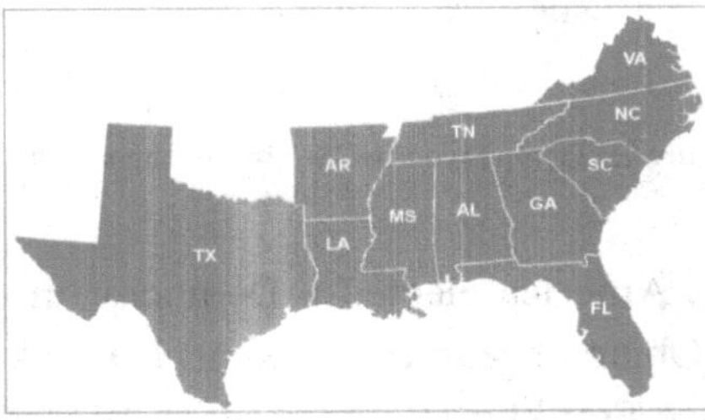

Figure 13: Bush Jr. swept the South in 2000 and 2004

In 2000, George W. Bush swept the South, just as his father had. The economy had come back from the recession left by his father. Clinton had not only substantially lowered unemployment but had balanced the budget for the first time in over seventy years.

The country was ripe to elect another Conservative as president. Remember, White Anxiety candidates get elected during good economies. Bush barely won the 2000 election, but he won just the same.

True to the idea of White Anxiety, Conservatives who run for office get elected during good economies. Also true to the cycle, Bush suffered two recessions. The last recession of his presidency, the Great Recession, left 7.8 percent unemployment, as his father had before him. George W. Bush left a $1.4 trillion deficit.

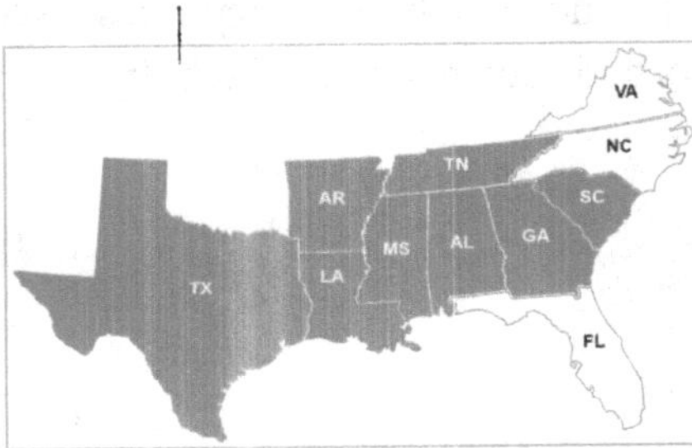

Figure 14: Obama won three Southern states in 2008

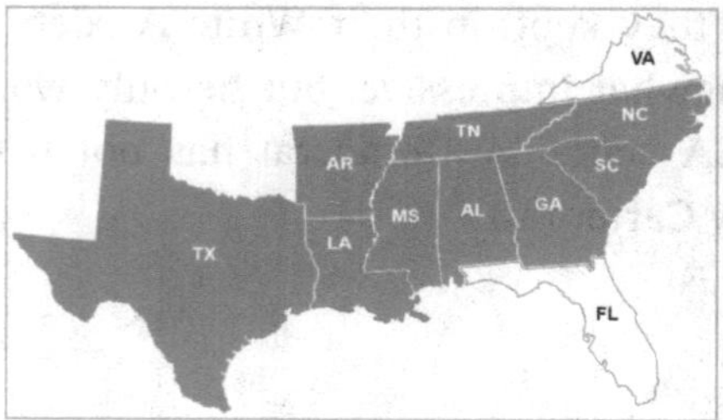

Figure 15: Obama won two Southern states in 2012

And, of course, America elected a Democrat in the next election. This time, Barack Obama became president. He took office during the worst economy since Franklin D. Roosevelt in 1932. Banks failed, foreclosures and bankruptcies broke records, and two of the Big Three automakers were in bankruptcy, headed for liquidation.

But still, even under those dire economic circumstances, Republicans nearly swept the former CSA states in the South. Obama won Florida, North Carolina, and Virginia in 2008. In the worst economy in seventy-six years, southern states still voted for Republicans, the party in power at the start of the recession.

Those southern states were locked in. Texas has not voted for a Democratic candidate for president in over thirty-two years. It did not matter how bad the economy turned, nor how badly their citizens were doing personally. They still voted for the Republican candidate in presidential elections.

Obama turned the economy around. He lowered the deficit by nearly 60 percent. He brought the unemployment rate down from 7.8 percent to 4.7 percent. By the time Obama left office, the health of our banks had returned to normal, bankruptcy rates were back to normal, and our automakers had returned to profitability.

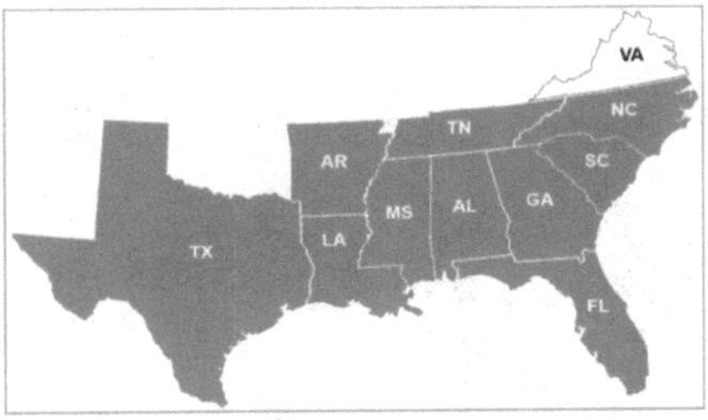

Figure 16: Donald Trump won the South in 2016

By the 2016 election, we had a good economy again. Most get it already—it's time for another White Anxiety candidate. This time, the candidate was Donald Trump.

Trump nearly swept the former CSA states in 2016, though, since Obama won Virginia, no Republican candidate has won it. However, Trump's message of states' rights and immigration reform helped him to win the rest of the South with White Anxiety voters.

After Trump took office in 2017, it seemed he really did not have much of a plan to govern the country. Perhaps he did not think he would win that election. His administration passed little new legislation. The economy went along as it had under Obama until Trump passed his first tax cut.

After that, the deficit began to rise significantly again. By the middle of Trump's term, the deficit had almost doubled. By the end of his term, due to a national emergency caused by the COVID pandemic, the deficit set a record. Trump left office with the largest deficit in American history—$2.7 trillion—and an unemployment rate of 6.4 percent. As the cycle goes, it was time to elect another Liberal as president. Remember, White Anxiety candidates rarely win elections after Republicans take the economy from good to bad. Democrats win elections when American voters find themselves in the midst of a poor economy.

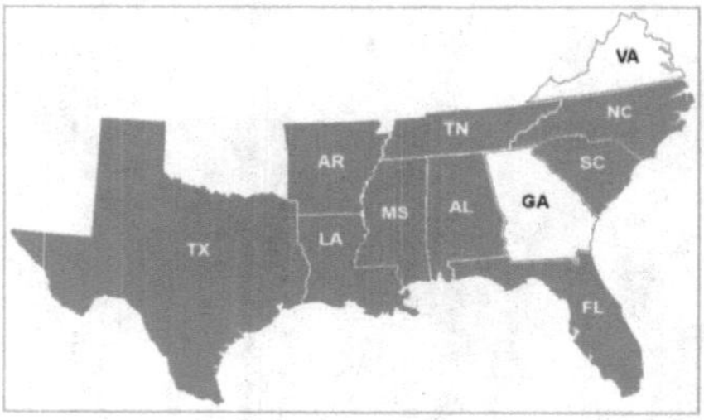

Figure 17: Biden won two southern states in 2020

Joe Biden won the 2020 election. He won only two former CSA states, Georgia and Virginia. In the previous election, Hillary Clinton had only won Virginia. As it stands, Virginia might be the first former CSA state to permanently turn away from White Anxiety politics. Georgia swings. Florida swings, but not so much. But Virginia has remained consistently objective since Obama's first election.

By the end of Biden's term, he left office with 4.0 percent unemployment and a $1.8 trillion deficit. The deficit, though still high, represents a 26 percent reduction from the deficit Trump left four years earlier.

America hadn't seen a president leave office with 4.0 percent or lower unemployment since Lyndon Johnson left office with 3.4 percent in 1969. Employment was strong, and the deficit continued to fall.

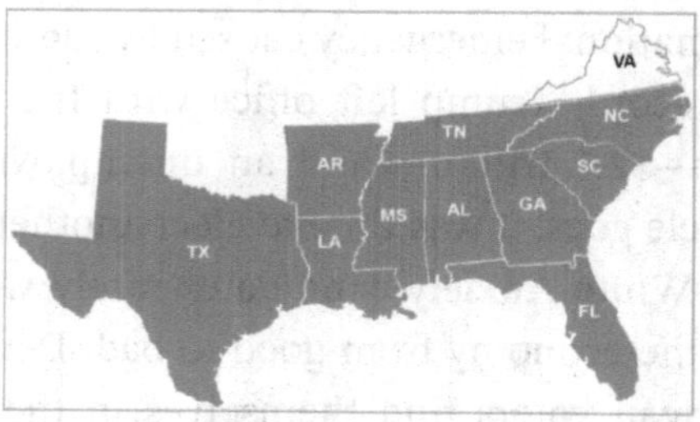

Figure 18: Trump won the South in 2024

Unfortunately, as I hope you are seeing from the pattern laid out so far, these are exactly the conditions under which White Anxiety thrives. Trump won the 2024 election.

So far, Trump's economic policies have taken the economy in the same direction that the policies of previous White Anxiety Conservative presidents have. Unemployment has risen; GDP growth has fallen. And the deficit is headed for a new record. But Trump's presidency isn't over yet, and there is no global crisis to blame.

However, in February 2026, Trump ordered the bombing of Iran. Iran immediately closed a transportation route crucial to oil delivery around the world, called the Strait of Hormuz. Since then, gas prices have risen significantly, and with them, inflation.

The pattern of White Anxiety should be clear.

WE SHOULD ALSO UNDERSTAND WHEN SOUTHERN BLACK PEOPLE STOPPED VOTING

Integral to the history of the former CSA states is the violent theft of voting rights from Black citizens. This practice, which began in the late 1860s, stripped a key component of citizenship from freed Black people. Despite all those instances of domestic violence, however, Black people used their intelligence and their newfound rights to rise in society.

To think, slavery ended in 1865. By 1872, Black citizens had elected candidates to Congress in nearly all the former Confederate states. Mississippi's legislature elected the first Black senator in America, Hiram Rhodes Revels. As mentioned previously, Black citizens helped elect Ulysses S. Grant. Black people had thriving farms and other businesses. Before the massacres, Black people had begun to live the American dream.

By 1876, White citizens in most of the southern states had violently hijacked elections from Black citizens. By the 1880s, once Conservatives were back in control, many southern states passed laws that stopped Black citizens of their states from even registering to vote. They used violence first, then laws, to make registering to vote almost impossible for Black people.

The history I've detailed here should help us to understand how we as a nation got where we are today. White Anxiety–fueled presidential candidates have done great harm to our economy. But they have also encouraged the fight against civil and voting rights for Black citizens.

Whenever we give an undue advantage to candidates for reasons outside of our economy, those candidates exploit that advantage. We give them no incentive to work in the interest of our country. After all, they won for reasons other than competence. They won to keep the perceived White Anxiety predators at bay.

We might believe that certain people can run our economy better than others. That idea might very well have merit. However, when we hire people who advocate for failed economic policy, we ignore merit. When we advocate for people who do not meet even minimal qualifications, we ignore merit. When we use tactics like violence, unfair registration, intimidation, and unfair district maps, we thwart merit.

White Anxiety candidates in the modern Republican Party took up the mantle left by modern Democrats. Once Democrats began to work to secure the civil and voting rights of Black citizens, modern Republicans stepped into the White Anxiety void they left.

If we continue to resort to long-standing tactics like White Anxiety, our country will continue to suffer one setback after another. At some point, we will have more setbacks than advances. And eventually, we will elect someone from whom we will not recover—if we haven't already.

Democratic administrations with pure growth since 1960

Joseph Biden

Barack Obama

Bill Clinton

Lyndon Johnson

John F Kennedy

Democratic presidential administrations during this period (1960–2026) under which the American economy produced growth without ever spawning a recession.

Republican administrations with pure growth since 1960

None

Republican presidential administrations during the same period (1960–2026) under which the American economy produced growth without ever spawning a recession.

CHAPTER 8
REPUBLICANS AND BAD ECONOMIES

> *They told all of us that Republican presidents and Republican Congresses exercise more fiscal discipline than Democratic presidents and Democratic Congresses. That is pants-on-fire false."*

CONSERVATIVE ECONOMICS BRINGS ABOUT RECESSIONS

I'M ALMOST ready for retirement, but in my entire lifetime, there has been only one Democratic administration that presided over a recession. In that same period, six Republican administrations presided over economies that produced ten recessions. "Lopsided" doesn't begin to capture it. We can find the shrapnel of our economy strewn over decades because of supply-side economics.

Conservatives who serve as presidents really do produce bad results. I know because I have lived through their presidencies. I was born in 1961, so I have lived through six Republican administrations. That means I have lived through ten recessions (the first two Eisenhower recessions happened before I was born).

Ronald Reagan campaigned on tamping down inflation, which had reached 14 percent under Jimmy Carter and was still at 11 percent when Reagan took office. He did bring it down. In the process, he spawned a pretty bad recession.

My father said to me during the Reagan recession that he would rather have a growing economy with high inflation than an economy in recession. He could figure out how to deal with high prices if he had a decent income.

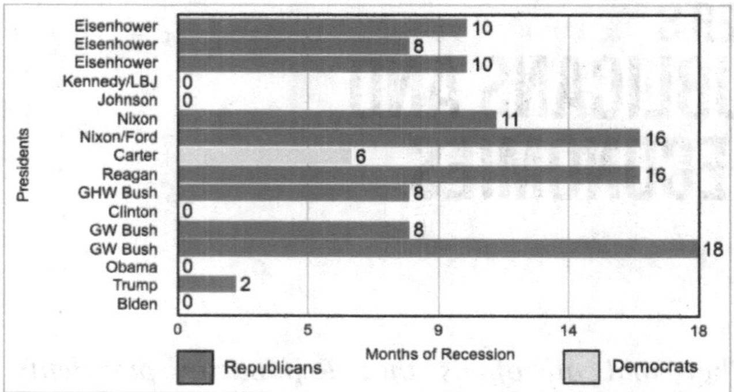

Figure 19: Presidents since 1953

During recessions, car sales decreased, and many of my father's customers were laid off. As I mentioned earlier, while my dad's customers were unemployed, they tended not to spend as much money on their cars. My father's business suffered during those times. And when my father's business suffered, my family suffered.

Not only that, but when the economy experienced a recession, our entire community and the rest of the city suffered. I can remember my next-door neighbor knocking on our front door one day. It was a cold fall day. His family was in need.

My mother always kept a garden. She and my dad grew up in North Carolina. Both grew up on farms. So, they both knew how to grow things. My father and his brothers worked on their family's farm as sharecroppers under their father. My father dropped out of school after the third grade to help his family work their farm.

My mother's fall crop of greens had come up well and sat there in our garden. I know very little about farming, but I did hear something about the frost hitting the greens. It had to do with frost making the greens taste sweeter—I'm not sure. Unfortunately, I never picked my mother's brain concerning the intricacies of growing vegetables. But the greens thrived there in her garden at the very back of our backyard.

So, our neighbor came by and asked if he could pick some of our greens. His family was hungry, and they had run out of money. They were a family of five.

This was the neighbor who worked for Cadillac. He had been laid off and was not sure when he would return to work. I'm sure he collected unemployment, but things were tough for everyone during those years. He picked the greens and fed his family.

When my father said he would rather have high inflation in a growing economy than low inflation in a recession, he made perfect sense. In Detroit, the bad economy brought on a frosty time for everyone, business owners as well as laborers. My father favored Democrats, though he did not vote. The Reagan recession that started in 1981 tied Nixon's second recession as the longest since the Great Depression of the 1930s. George W. Bush's second recession, otherwise known as the Great Recession, which started in December of 2007, now holds that record.

DEMOCRATIC ECONOMICS BRING ABOUT GROWTH

I'm including these statistics to make a point. Everything I've charted in this chapter comes from government websites. The Bureau of Labor Statistics has tracked the unemployment rate every month since January 1948. They have missed only one month since they started. That month was October 2025 under the Donald Trump administration. Imagine that. Through wars, shutdowns, a pandemic, and other challenges, the Bureau of Labor Statistics had never missed a month until the second Trump administration.

If we based our decision to elect a president on actual performance, we would force any Republican candidate for president to face these lopsided statistics. Those Conservatives who aspire to the office of the president would need to assure us that they would not use the same economic philosophy as previous Conservatives who ran our economy as presidents.

But if we make our decision to elect a president based on White Anxiety driven by Conservatives, we should prepare ourselves for the same outcomes we have always experienced when Conservatives serve as president.

Yet, with this stark comparison data, polling up until the 2024 election suggested—or even proved—that Americans believed that the economy works better under Republicans than Democrats. Victims of White Anxiety need to believe that. So Republican candidates, knowing the truth about their economies, reassure their voters with all the lies necessary to keep them happy about their votes. After all, they did not pick Republican candidates for their economic prowess. They picked those candidates to save them from the anxieties that Republicans pushed on them.

REPUBLICANS' ECONOMICS STIFLE JOB GROWTH

This is another example of a stark difference in how the economy performs under Democratic administrations versus how it performs under Republican administrations. Productive economies have low unemployment rates. Economies with stagnant growth and economies in recession—that is, those with negative growth rates—have higher unemployment rates.

Bad economies are bad for middle- and lower-income citizens, as the loss of a job, coupled with poor prospects for finding another, can mean a change in a family's lifestyle. A robust American economy benefits Democrats and Republicans alike.

DEFICITS MATTER

As mentioned previously, a deficit occurs when we spend more than we take in. We have a surplus when we spend less than we take in. The larger the deficit, the faster we accumulate debt. The smaller the deficit, the slower we accumulate debt.

During my lifetime, only one president has eliminated America's budget deficit. He stopped increasing the deficit, lowered it, eliminated it, and generated a surplus. Bill Clinton caused our federal budget to reach surplus status in the second year of his second term as president. To get there, Clinton signed the Omnibus Budget Reconciliation Act of 1993, also known as the Balanced Budget Act of 1993.

The Balanced Budget Act lowered our deficit by Clinton's second year in office. The deficit continued to diminish every year of his first term. By his second term, the budget was balanced. In 1998, the budget went from deficit to surplus. By the time Clinton left office, the country was well on its way to eliminating our national debt.

The difference in the performance of Democrats and Republicans when it comes to the deficit is stark. The list below points out facts about the disparity.

1. The most recent Democratic administrations to leave office with a lower deficit than when they entered office:
    - *Joe Biden (2021–2025): $2 trillion*
    - *Barack Obama (2009–2017): $587 billion*
    - *Bill Clinton (1993–2001): $236 billion* ***surplus***

2. The most recent Republican administrations to leave office with a lower deficit than when they entered office:
    - *Calvin Coolidge (1923-1929): $185 million* ***surplus***

3. Presidential administration to leave office with the largest federal deficit:
    - *Donald Trump (2021): $2.7 trillion*

4. Presidential administration to leave office with the largest percentage increase in the national debt:
    - *Ronald Reagan (1989): 189 percent*

5. Presidential administration to leave office with the largest surplus:
    - *Bill Clinton (2001): $236 billion*

Again, there is no real comparison. Republicans have a consistent track record of failure at running America's economy.

OUR TRUST MATTERS

In recent decades, America faced a crisis in the Catholic Church. Catholic parishioners discovered that priests had molested their children for generations. Previously, unless someone had personally experienced sexual abuse by Catholic priests, they would have had no reason to suspect them. They would most likely have felt comfortable leaving their young male children with priests.

Would they have had such a comfort level with leaving their children with just anyone? No. But priests had a title that allayed their fears. Since priests had that title, they assumed their personalities and values would align with it. They might consider them "men of God" without a second thought. People tend to look at priests as men with high moral values.

They would expect priests to live up to their office. Based on that expectation, they might assume that they would not do anything to damage their children psychologically for life, like child molestation. For many Catholics, that expectation was wrong.

Priests molested altar boys at an alarming rate. They did not get away with it for decades because parents were irresponsible. They got away with it because what the parents knew for sure just was not so. Remember the saying we discussed earlier: "It ain't what you do not know that gets you in trouble. It's what you know for sure that just ain't so."

WE CANNOT TRUST POLITICIANS

Our founding fathers built the U.S. government around the expectation that people do not always do the right thing. In fact, they went a step further. They expected that people would do the *wrong* thing.

So they set up a government based on a lack of trust. They made each branch of government accountable to another. And they ultimately made all branches accountable to the people. That means we have an important role to play in keeping our government honest. No one should get our stamp of approval or our vote unless they prove they are worthy.

When we trust an institution implicitly, we open ourselves up to injury. In the case of the Catholic Church, its priests molested children, according to court cases.[i] They enjoyed the trust of their parishioners. They abused that trust.

Republicans have gotten away with a similar deception for decades. As I said before, the title "Conservative" can mean anything they want it to mean. And Republicans have added many philosophies and practices to that title. Conservative fiscal policy is one of them. They might say, "We want to cut out waste, fraud, and abuse and lower spending." That sounds fiscally conservative. They might call themselves "pro-life." That sounds religiously conservative.

But nearly all those assertions are false. As I write this book, the three branches of government are completely controlled by Republicans. Republicans hold majorities in the House of Representatives and the Senate. The president of the United States is also a Republican. The chief justice of the Supreme Court is a Republican, and most of the justices are Republicans.

The voting public believes that Republicans manage the economy better than Democrats. The voters did not reach that conclusion because each voter researched the history of American macroeconomics. They did not come to that conclusion by watching an economist truthfully and extensively present an analysis of the economic results of Republican administrations juxtaposed with those of Democrats. That did not happen.

Americans fell for the same trick as Catholic parishioners. Just because the Republican Party has the title of "political party" does not mean their candidates know anything about running the government. Belonging to a party that has not had a president leave office with a lower deficit in more than ninety years should make them the underdog in any election. Americans should demand economic competence in their political leaders. Our financial lives, in many cases, depend on their competence.

Americans did not even check. Many Republicans voted based on feelings and party loyalty. They had no idea what voting for a Conservative to run our government meant. Unfortunately, many of them did not know what Conservatives advocate for in terms of fiscal policy. They have no idea what Conservatives think of our federal government. Many cannot tell us why they call themselves Conservatives. They probably know little or nothing about the effects of supply-side economics.

Maybe "conservative" just sounds good. Perhaps being "a Conservative" is what their corner of society expects from them.

American voters concluded that Republicans run our economy well because Republican candidates and party operatives told them so. They told all of us that Republican presidents and Republican Congresses exercise more fiscal discipline than Democratic presidents and Democratic Congresses. That is pants-on-fire false. We can see that in the data.

In 2025, the first year of Donald Trump's second term, the federal government spent more money than it spent in 2024. Yet the pundits of Conservatives continued to tell us that the Trump administration saved us money by reducing the federal government's head count. The sum total of all federal employees' salaries and benefits represent only about 5 percent of the federal budget. Heck, in 2026, interest on the national debt represents about 17 percent of the federal budget. Based on the math, cutting federal workers did not represent a serious attempt at fiscal discipline.

Republican voters knew "for sure" that Trump would lower inflation, cut the deficit, and produce a better economy than Kamala Harris would. They knew that without a doubt, because Republicans told them that. They willingly accepted Republicans' claims at face value. They did not feel they had to check the party's assertions against history.

During the 2024 election, voters could have looked at data from Trump's first-term before they trusted what he told them. Republicans only told them what they wanted to hear. Many of their supporters knew better. But they wanted what they wanted. And the more that friends and relatives warned them, the more they wanted Conservatives. Voters acted like a young daughter introducing her parents to her new ex-felon boyfriend. The more her parents objected, the more she clung to him.

REAGANOMICS: THE ALBATROSS AROUND THE NECK OF THE AMERICAN ECONOMY

When Ronald Reagan ran for president in 1980, George H. W. Bush ran against him in the Republican presidential primary. During the primary, Reagan put forward his plan for massive tax cuts. He would eventually lower the highest tax rate from 70 percent to 28 percent by the time he left office. Reagan explained that reducing the federal tax burden on wealthy Americans and corporations would spur massive economic growth. He also cloaked the policy in a tax break for the lowest-income Americans.[ii] As mentioned previously, Bush called Reagan's plan "voodoo economics."[iii] Bush explained that Reagan's plan to reduce tax rates would result in huge budget deficits for years to come. Reagan would not budge. What we now call Reaganomics was built on the idea that giving more money to the wealthy benefits everyone in the economy. Cutting their taxes would put more money in their pockets. Their spending would eventually trickle down to everyone below them, boosting the entire economy.

Before Reaganomics, the world considered America a lender nation. Our banks lent more money to other nations than America borrowed from other nations. Since Reagan, America has become a debtor nation. America's annual federal budget deficits have risen during every Republican president's tenure, dating back to the 1930s. Reagan still holds the record for the largest percentage increase of the national debt during a single president's tenure in office. The national debt increased by 189 percent from Ronald Reagan's 1981 inauguration until his 1989 departure. That means the national debt almost tripled in that time.

Reaganomics implemented supply-side economics. Arthur B. Laffer developed the idea that lowering tax rates would stimulate economic growth and increase tax revenues. Laffer advised Ronald Reagan and Donald Trump on their economic plans. Reagan's economic plan brought about massive deficits and debt. America's economy under Trump's plan performed equally poorly.

After Reagan served two terms, George H. W. Bush, Reagan's vice president, won the 1988 election. Bush had promised not to raise taxes during his campaign. However, as the deficit began to rise, he could not deny that his prediction of deficits and debt as far as the eye could see had come true.

Probably against his better political judgment, Bush decided to sign a bill that would raise taxes on top income earners. Bush made a smart economic decision for the nation, but the decision did not work out well for him politically.

Pat Buchanan challenged Bush Sr. in the 1992 Republican presidential primary on that very idea. Bush won the primary, but Buchanan had severely wounded him. Buchanan forced Bush to appeal to White Anxiety. Bush's southern strategy won all the 36°30′ states, along with Idaho, Indiana, Kansas, Utah, and Wyoming, but Bush lost the election to a real southerner, Bill Clinton, from Arkansas.

After Reagan, America never returned to a 70 percent tax bracket for high income earners. The highest income tax bracket has remained under 50 percent. This massive change in the income tax rate for the wealthiest Americans has enabled them to accumulate wealth, with a growing number of billionaires.

Reagan used White Anxiety to win the election. Then, after he entered office, he caused the worst recession of my adult life. As I mentioned earlier, I got married in 1983. Although I maintained steady employment, many of my friends suffered financial ruin during those years. In fact, I moved from Detroit to a city in the Southwest because Detroit's economy was toast.

Trusting Republicans to run the economy, after the track record I just laid out, is just a bad idea. We should never let irresponsible, unqualified people with a bad track record, who we know are using a failed philosophy, manage our finances just because they appealed to our emotions. We should expect more from the people we entrust with our precious vote.

CHAPTER 9
POOR PERFORMANCE AND BAD BEHAVIOR

> “*Not only does the entire country suffer when America elects a Republican as president, but the states that Republicans count on to win seem to suffer the most.*”

EMPLOYING White Anxiety to win elections affords Conservatives the luxury of having no performance requirements. Sure, they make performance promises during their campaigns. But they suffer no negative consequences when they fail to deliver on those promises. In many cases, they pretend to have delivered, even when they did not.

Their constituents do not seem to mind very much, though. They do not vote for candidates who will help the government run the economy better, keep us safe, or employ the government to do big things, things too big for any one company or state to accomplish.

They seem to vote for candidates who will keep the social order they want and protect them from those they see as predators: non-White people and immigrants.

Since Republicans want to keep their candidates in power, they cannot really complain or withdraw their votes. After all, who will fulfill their emotional needs like those candidates? Also, they have ruled out voting for candidates from the party of Liberals, Democrats. So, no matter how badly Republicans affect the economy and even their own lives, they must justify the acts of Republican politicians and continue to vote for them.

Conservatives do that by ignoring poor performance. They fool themselves and try to fool others into thinking the bad economy is the media's creation. And many times, Conservatives pretend that a bad economy is good. Conservative politicians use many tools to normalize poor performance. White Anxiety is just one of them.

I first experienced this phenomenon under George H. W. Bush. Back then, as I mentioned earlier, I listened to the late Rush Limbaugh. I did not agree with his policy ideas. After all, he was a Conservative, and I am a Liberal. But Rush was an interesting fellow and very entertaining. But, most importantly, I relied on Rush to help me understand how Conservatives thought.

When the economy entered a recession under Bush Sr., Rush presented stat after stat to portray a good economy, despite what the government and economists were telling his listeners. By the time Bush ran against Clinton, the unemployment rate had risen from the 5.4 percent rate Bush inherited from Ronald Reagan to 7.4 percent. America had gone deep into recession. And Rush still said everything was alright. Well, Rush did well, no matter what happened. Rush made over $10 million a year with his EIB Network. Rush Limbaugh was the most popular radio talk show host in American history. The economy had gone into recession, just as economic data indicated.

Here are a few things we know about the states that voted for Ronald Reagan and most other Republican presidential candidates since:

- Nine of the ten poorest states voted for Republican presidents.
- Nine of the ten states with the lowest GDP per capita voted for Republican presidents.
- Eight of the ten states with the highest infant mortality rates voted for Republican presidents.
- The top five states with the highest healthcare uninsured rate voted for Republican presidents.

Not only does the entire country suffer when America elects a Republican as president, but the states that Republicans count on to win seem to suffer the most.

Those states have poorer citizens, produce less, experience some of the worst medical outcomes, and have some of the lowest rates of medical insurance. I did not intend this list to be an exhaustive account of the ills these former Confederate states suffer because of White Anxiety. I wanted to illustrate how their decision to support underperforming presidents produces negative outcomes simply because those campaigns trigger their White Anxiety.

Because they vote based on emotion, they accept underperformance. But they also accept bad behavior. From Richard Nixon to Donald Trump, all these White Anxiety–elected presidents displayed bad behavior.

RICHARD NIXON, THE ONLY PRESIDENT TO RESIGN FROM OFFICE

Richard Nixon resigned from office after the House started impeachment proceedings. Republicans in the Senate assured Nixon that the Senate would vote to remove him from office if the House impeached him. The House of Representatives decided to start impeachment proceedings after listening to the evidence against the Watergate Hotel break-in crew. Through the release of White House tapes, the House discovered that Nixon had a direct influence on the cover-up of the break-in. Nixon resigned from office on August 7, 1974. He is the only president to ever resign from office.

But the corruption of the Nixon administration did not stop there. The State of Maryland and, eventually, the Department of Justice investigated Nixon's vice president, Spiro Agnew. His investigation ran parallel to the Watergate investigation of Nixon. Agnew and Nixon were in the news daily as their respective investigations progressed.

Agnew resigned his office and accepted his plea deal by pleading nolo contendere to one felony count of tax evasion on that same day. He received a sentence of three years of unsupervised probation and a

$10,000 fine. John C. Calhoun was the only other vice president of the United States to resign from office; he resigned in 1932.

RONALD REAGAN CAME CLEAN ON ILLEGALITY

Ronald Reagan may have broken the law. But he skirted prosecution by apologizing.

The scandal was called the Iran–Contra Affair. Congress had passed, and Reagan had signed, the Boland Amendments. This series of laws restricted funding to the Contras in Nicaragua.

Reagan sold weapons to Iran. In the process, he may have violated the Arms Export Control Act. He sold those weapons to secure the release of Americans held hostage by Hezbollah in Lebanon. The Boland Amendments made it illegal for the U.S. Treasury to fund the Contras in Nicaragua. However, to circumvent those laws, the Reagan administration secretly sold weapons to Iran and used the proceeds from those sales to fund the Contras, in direct violation of the Boland Amendments.

At first, Reagan denied that his administration officials had participated in breaking the law by selling weapons for hostages. Later, on March 4, 1987, Reagan came clean and admitted that his administration had traded arms for hostages.

Several members of his administration were indicted, tried, and convicted of various crimes. George H. W. Bush, Reagan's vice president, pardoned those whom the Justice Department prosecuted and convicted. Neither Reagan nor Bush was impeached or otherwise prosecuted. Sound familiar?

GEORGE W. BUSH AND THE IRAQ WMD SCANDAL

First, George W. Bush started the Iraq War on the pretense that Iraq had weapons of mass destruction (WMD). Bush said that Iraq possessed nuclear weapons that it did not have.

Most major countries, including France, Germany, and Italy, refused to participate in the invasion of Iraq. They did not believe Bush had made his case when he presented evidence of WMDs. Bush called the group of countries that agreed to send troops to Iraq "the Coalition of the Willing." Forty-eight countries, along with the United States, sent troops and other military support to fight against Iraq. The UK was the only other major power that participated in that coalition.

Even though forty-nine total countries participated in the Iraq War, they did so symbolically. The United States sent 80 percent of the troops. American troops represented 93 percent of the deaths of coalition forces during the war. The countries that made up the coalition of the willing added their countries to the list of countries that supported the war, but most of them sent no troops.

Most major powers had serious doubts about the WMD claims by the Bush administration for good reason. Bush's claims were not backed up by solid evidence. Most of them decided they would not put their troops' lives on the line to back up what was, at best, incompetence and was, at worst, a lie.

The Bush administration never found WMD in Iraq. This became a major scandal in America. The Senate Intelligence Committee conducted hearings on WMD claims and found them just short of fraudulent. They concluded that the claims did not justify America going to war.

DONALD TRUMP SUFFERED TWO IMPEACHMENTS

Donald Trump holds the distinction of being the only president in American history who the House of Representatives impeached twice. Trump is also the only president to have members of his own party vote to remove him from office in the Senate.

Ten Republican senators voted for Trump's removal from office. Notice that I did not say "after his trial in the Senate." He did not have a trial in the Senate either time. Well, officially, he did have a trial. History will record it that way. But, if we use the actual definition of a trial, he did not have one either time.

After the House of Representatives impeached Trump, the Senate took up its responsibility to hold a trial. However, the Republican-controlled Senate voted not to hear from any witnesses. Senate

Republicans also voted against allowing the prosecution or defense to present any exhibits or evidence.

A trial, as the name suggests, tries charges made by an authority against witnesses and evidence. A trial is a search for the truth. "Verdict" means "a true writing" in Latin. Trials require that the triers of fact weigh charges presented by the prosecution against evidence and sworn witnesses. If a so-called trial has no evidence and no witnesses, it is not a trial. There is nothing to try.

In an impeachment trial in the Senate, the House is the charging authority. When the House votes to impeach, they, in effect, indict the president with one or more high crimes, one or more misdemeanors, or a mixture of both. After the impeachment, the Senate becomes the triers of fact.

Republicans controlled the Senate. They shamelessly voted against putting Trump on trial in the real sense. What Republicans called a trial in the Senate was simply opening and closing statements by the defense and the prosecution. Also, most of the Senate Republicans who voted to remove the president from office lost their next reelection campaigns. They broke the rules of White Anxiety—similar to Bush Sr.

TRUMP'S FIRST IMPEACHMENT

Donald Trump was charged with the following in his first impeachment:

- Soliciting help from Ukraine during the 2020 election by asking them to open an investigation against Joe Biden during the 2020 campaign. Ukraine's president refused to open the investigation.
- Conditioning official acts (selling of weapons to Ukraine authorized by Congress) on Ukraine opening that investigation.

The two formal charges in the articles were:

1. Abuse of power
2. Obstruction of Congress

The House Judiciary Committee passed articles of impeachment out of committee on a party-line vote. The vote on the floor passed with two and three Democratic defections on each article, respectively.

In the Senate, after the mock trial, Mitt Romney made history as the first member of the Senate of an impeached president's own party to vote for his removal from office.

THE RESULT OF LETTING THINGS RIDE

Unpunished crime emboldens the next actor. Each time a president escapes accountability, the next one pushes further. By the time we reach Donald Trump, we have arrived at an entirely new level of corruption, one decades in the making.

White Anxiety is what makes that escape possible. Those who voted for Conservatives didn't simply elect them to govern—they also elected Conservatives to protect them from the "others." Bad outcomes get blamed on the previous administration. The excuse never changes.

The Constitution gives no president special permission to ignore the law. Article I makes clear that a president remains liable for prosecution after leaving office. We must hold them accountable—every one of them, regardless of party.

Mitch McConnell, the Republican Senate Majority Leader at the time of both impeachment trials, gave a long speech justifying the actions of the Senate in not convicting Trump for his crimes. McConnell argued that the Senate could not vote to convict and remove the president since he was no longer in office. That was a shameful technicality. At the time the House handed up the impeachment (indictment), Trump was president. McConnell went on to say that the Department of Justice (DOJ) could still try Trump for his crimes. The DOJ under Joe Biden, with the help of a special prosecutor, indicted Trump for multiple crimes. Trials for those crimes never took place before Trump won a second term.

We learned after Trump's second term started that he had retaliated against employees of the DOJ who worked on his prosecution. Trump worked to make sure that his attorney general found and fired prosecutors and agents who worked on the Trump investigations and prosecutions. Trump also threatened to prosecute all members of Congress who participated in the January 6th Committee investigation and presentation to the country.

Voters embolden successful White Anxiety candidates. Trump knew that he would not receive any significant pushback from his voters.

Figure 20 displays a list of administrations since 1969, along with indictments and convictions of administration officials.

Indictments and convictions of administration officials

Administration	Years	Indictments	Convictions
Nixon/Ford	1969-1977	76	55
Carter	1977-1981	1	0
Reagan	1981-1989	26	16
GHW Bush	1989-1993	1	1
Clinton	1993-2001	2	1
GW Bush	2001-2009	16	16
Obama	2009-2017	0	0
Trump	2017-2021	199	8
Biden	2021-2025	0	0
Total Republican		318	96
Total Democratic		3	1

Figure 20

Figure 20: Indictments and convictions of Administration officials (*A-Mark Foundation U.S. Presidents and the Federal Deficit - February 3, 2023*)

Total indictments and convictions:

Democratic administrations: Indictments: 3, Convictions: 1

Republican administrations: Indictments: 318, Convictions: 96

The comparison is not close. When people know they can get away with criminality without consequences, we will see more criminality. The numbers also speak to Republicans' lack of respect for government and the rule of law. Since, in the eyes of Republicans, the government is the problem, they believe it is already corrupt—so their approach to governing reflects that lack of respect.

The truth is that the government is not inherently corrupt. As Figure 20 shows, not every president's administration commits a crime.

David wrote in the book of Psalms: "I said in my haste, All men are liars."[i] David suggests he made this pronouncement hastily, but it seems he realized it was inaccurate. Indeed, not all men are liars. When we assume we can get away with certain things because "all men" do them, we abandon what we know to be right in favor of what we think others do. That is dangerous.

VOTE FOR CANDIDATES WITH INTEGRITY

When we allow candidates to tug at our emotions over a long period of time, we get bad outcomes. Figure 21 shows that eight of the ten states with the highest poverty rates in the nation are states that reliably vote for presidential candidates who are Conservatives. Seven of those ten states also have Republicans serving as their governors.

As shown in Figure 22, in 2025, we see that nine out of the ten states with the highest number of citizens without health insurance voted Republican for president. Eight of those ten states have Republican governors.

We can observe a pattern: Republican voters tolerate underperforming presidents and governors. They seem content to remain in poverty with limited health insurance options. Of course, they are—they rarely demand much from Republican leaders. Why? Because Republicans understand that they have these voters' allegiance due to White Anxiety. Candidates know they have conditioned Republican voters to support them regardless of performance or potential criminal behavior.

States with highest poverty rates

State	Poverty Rate	Party for President	Party of Governor
Louisiana	18.9%	Republican	Republican
Mississippi	18.0%	Republican	Republican
New Mexico	17.8%	Democratic	Democratic
West Virginia	16.7%	Republican	Republican
Kentucky	16.4%	Republican	Democratic
Oklahoma	15.9%	Republican	Republican
Arkansas	15.7%	Republican	Republican
Alabama	15.6%	Republican	Republican
New York	14.2%	Democratic	Democratic

Figure 21

Figure 21: States with the highest poverty rates

States with highest healthcare uninsured rates

State	Uninsured rate	Party for President	Party of Governor
Texas	16.7%	Republican	Republican
Georgia	12.0%	Republican	Republican
Oklahoma	11.5%	Republican	Republican
Nevada	11.4%	Republican	Republican
Alaska	11.0%	Republican	Republican
Florida	10.9%	Republican	Republican
Wyoming	10.3%	Republican	Republican
Arizona	10.3%	Republican	Democratic
New Mexico	10.1%	Democratic	Democratic

Figure 22

Figure 22: States with the highest healthcare uninsured rates

Republican voters now appear to anticipate poor performance, possibly preferring recessions under Republican presidents over growing economies under Democratic ones. As with many concepts, this may seem acceptable until it actually occurs.

Once we suffer a recession, complete with job losses and other economic disasters, some rush to elect a Democratic president. Others would rather stay home than vote beyond the bounds of White Anxiety. They feel good about throwing the Republican out who brought about the recession. That is, until the next White Anxiety candidate comes along, assuring them once again that he will save them from the "other."

CHAPTER 10
CONSERVATIVES MUST COME CLEAN

> "*Bush started his presidency with a $236 billion surplus left by Bill Clinton, the largest federal budget surplus—the only budget surplus—in eighty years. In eight years, Bush turned that massive surplus into what was, at the time, the largest deficit in American history.*"

RECESSIONS ARE NOT CYCLICAL

CONSERVATIVES OFTEN OFFER various excuses for why Republican administrations tend to trigger economic recessions. The media frequently questions them on this point, as their policies invariably lead us into recession. Their usual response is to provide excuses, which are essentially lies disguised as reasoning. And when I say "every time," I mean *every single* instance. Since Eisenhower, Republican administrations have experienced an average of one recession per four-year presidential term.

Here are a few of the excuses (lies) Conservatives give for recessions:

1. Recessions are cyclical. They come around periodically no

matter what economic policy we execute. It's not Republicans' fault.

2. Republican recessions are just delayed effects of Democratic administration policies that preceded Republican administrations. It's not Republicans' fault.
3. Economists are unfairly quick to mark a recession under Republican administrations. It's not Republicans' fault.

If any of those excuses contained a modicum of truth, more Democratic administrations would have presided over economies that spawned recessions. Some Republican administrations—the ones that lasted eight years—spawned two recessions. Not a single two-term modern Democratic administration has overseen an economy that spawned a single recession in nearly the last half-century.

So, what's the difference between the two economies? As I said, I'm a software engineer, not an economist. But I've observed a few things.

- Republicans believe their own ideology in place of sound economic policy.
- Republicans have a conservative view of the national government; to them, government is useless except for its military.
- Republicans believe that Democrats do not know how to run the government.
- Republicans do not believe in the power of a nation working together under a unified government. They have disdain for the federal government.
- When Republicans gain power using deception, it's awfully hard to transition to honesty.
- Dishonesty breeds criminality.
- Criminality engenders irresponsibility.

CONSERVATIVES TAKE BOLD IDEOLOGICAL STEPS

Ronald Reagan took office when I was in college. When he won the 1980 election, he immediately froze hiring of all federal government personnel. Why would I remember that? I had worked for the Army Corps of Engineers since the eleventh grade. I looked forward to working for the Corps of Engineers in the summer of 1981. But my manager at the Corps of Engineers in Detroit informed me, while I was still attending college that semester, that there might not be a job for me when I returned for the summer.

What's the point? Conservatives take bold ideological steps when they enter office. George W. Bush immediately passed a tax cut in his first six months after taking office. Bush immediately turned the $236 billion budget surplus that Bill Clinton had built over his two terms into a budget deficit before the first year of his presidency ended.

I remember the lengthy recount and court cases after the 2000 Bush–Gore election. I stayed up the night the Supreme Court handed down the Bush v. Gore decision. Heartbroken, I read the ruling until 2 a.m. that morning. I could not believe that the Supreme Court, in which I had so much faith, had made such a partisan and cowardly decision.

For many years, until he died in 2016, Antonin Scalia's only comment on the Bush v. Gore decision was "Get over it."[i] No legal arguments. No references to precedent. No lengthy, originalist manifesto—just "Get over it." How shameful.

Anyway, I thought our saving grace was that Republicans controlled both houses and the presidency. If they screwed this up, they would have to answer to the American people.

REPUBLICANS ARE NOT HELD ACCOUNTABLE WHEN THOSE BOLD STEPS FAIL

After Bush Jr.'s bold steps, the economy was severely destabilized. It was damaged to such an extent that it resulted in the most severe economic downturn since the Great Depression. By 2007, Bush and Congress had implemented three tax cuts, initiated two wars, and generated what was, at the time, the largest annual budget deficit in American history.

Another thing I recall is that, leading up to the 2008 election, the economy had clearly deteriorated. In Detroit, several of the people I knew got pink slips. The CEOs of the automotive industry visited Washington with humble requests for financial assistance. Two of the three major automakers had already filed for bankruptcy.

However, this period saw the economy and poor decision-making accelerate their decline toward potential liquidation. The United States also experienced a liquidity crisis, with banks failing and individuals losing their homes. This was the most challenging economic period I have ever witnessed. The signs of recession were evident throughout the country.

But this time was different. No official agency had declared a recession, despite the obvious signs. I listened to the news constantly, wondering when they would officially call it. On December 1, 2008, the National Bureau of Economic Research (NBER) announced that the U.S. economy had experienced negative growth, officially confirming a recession that had begun in December 2007.

So, we went through the entire 2008 presidential campaign during this recession. And although the downturn had started under the party in power, they faced no immediate blame during the campaign. The Bush administration had triggered a second recession. Even though Americans were suffering, NBER waited until *after* the presidential election to declare a recession that had already been ongoing for a year.

And then the Conservatives began blaming Bill Clinton. Clinton had left office nearly eight years earlier. They said Clinton forced banks to lend to anyone with a pulse through the Community Reinvestment Act. The Community Reinvestment Act did not force banks to lend or even cause banks to make mortgage loans irresponsibly.

Collateralized debt obligations (CDOs) caused banks to make massive amounts of high-risk loans. The banks made bad loans so they could bundle them into CDOs and sell them to investors. CDOs had insane markups as AAA investments. The movie *The Big Short* outlined that crisis rather dramatically.

Again, Republicans devised a way to wiggle out of taking responsibility for an economic disaster. When Bush left office, he left the worst economy in eighty years. Bush also saddled Barack Obama's administration with what was, at the time, the largest deficit in American history, $1.4 trillion, along with that horrific economy.

Bush started his presidency with a $236 billion surplus left by Bill Clinton, the largest federal budget surplus—the only budget surplus—in eighty years. In eight years, Bush turned that massive surplus into what was, at the time, the largest deficit in American history. Imagine that. Liberals leave a surplus, and Conservatives turn it into a deficit after they gain control of the presidency and both houses of Congress. Republicans lie about the spending reputation of Democrats. They also lie about their own spending.

AND THEN DEMOCRATS CLEAN UP THE MESS

Barack Obama's administration would turn that horrible situation around over the next eight years. Obama took office with a 7.8 percent unemployment rate and a $1.4 trillion annual federal deficit. Bank failures, home foreclosures, and bankruptcies topped record highs. Two of the Big Three automakers in Detroit had declared bankruptcy and seemed headed for liquidation. The unemployment rate was over 8 percent after Obama's first few weeks in office. It would rise to 10 percent before it began to fall. The Dow Jones Industrial Average was at 7,949.09. Bill Clinton left the Dow at $10,600 in January 2001, when Bush took office. The Bush administration brought about the worst economic downturn since the Great Depression.

Obama left office with 4.7 percent unemployment, an annual federal budget deficit of $587 billion, and a Dow Jones Industrial Average around 19,800.

But guess what? Polling during the Hillary Clinton campaign—the next presidential election campaign—found that voters thought Republicans did a better job with the economy than Democrats. What? Why, after all that, would voters not get it? Why would they not understand that a Republican administration, after eight years, had left the worst economy in eighty years? Because Republicans told them differently. And, without effective messaging from Democrats, they believed Republicans.

During the Bush administration, America started two wars. For the first time in American history, the federal government did not raise taxes to pay for its wars. Bush increased overall spending and cut federal taxes three times in eight years. Bush, along with the Republican Congress, acted irresponsibly by giving tax cuts during two armed conflicts overseas. All in all, the Iraq War is estimated to have cost over $2 trillion. The War in Afghanistan is estimated to have cost $4 trillion.

THE TRUTH IS THE ONLY WAY TO COUNTER EXCUSES

We have covered a lot of ground. But some things bear repeating—not because the case needs more making (I've shown the receipts and the evidence has been in for nearly a century), but because these facts should be impossible to forget:

Republicans will keep making excuses for their economic record as long as we let them. Democrats will keep losing the messaging war as long as they refuse to fight it. And American voters will keep suffering the consequences as long as they don't know what I've laid out in this book.

I understand that when Democrats are out of power, they focus on getting back in so they can fix the damage. That's honorable. But it leaves the floor open to the spin of Conservatives. For the good of all Americans, Democrats must tell the truth before, during, and after every economic disaster—and get ahead of the excuses before they take root.

Because here is what everyone should know—and what too few do:

- Every Republican administration for nearly the last century has averaged one recession per four-year term.
- No Republican administration has left office with unemployment below 5 percent since 1929.
- Every Republican administration in nearly the last century has left office with a larger deficit than it inherited.
- Republicans tank the economy every time because they keep trying to make supply-side—voodoo—economics work.

- Republicans focus legislation on helping the wealthy at the expense of everyone else.

WE MUST MAKE THEM PAY

Knowing that the economic philosophies of Conservatives don't work is only half the battle. The truth is that we need Conservatives to find a philosophy and economic model that work. One-party rule won't work either, at least not for long. If a single party believes it will never lose, it won't feel accountable to its electorate anymore. And then, instead of pointing out how Republicans can get away with anything and still get elected, we will have that problem with Democrats.

We certainly need to take the Conservatives to the woodshed, as the old folks would say. But we should not take them there to shoot them in the head and leave them for dead.

As a country, we need two productive parties, two equally responsible parties. The idea of limited government can work alongside a party that wants to use the advantage of government to accomplish big things for our country.

As long as neither party goes too far in either direction, the two parties can work to ensure that our republic thrives. The first step toward that new world is the Republican Party's reckoning. The voters must make that happen.

CHAPTER 11
WEALTH CONCENTRATION HURTS US ALL

> *Risk-taking was not the only factor that helped bring about the Great Depression. Hoarding wealth created the environment for that massive risk-taking."*

IN 1983, Ronald Reagan cut the highest tax rate from 70 percent down to 50 percent. Republicans would eventually lower the highest tax rate again to 28 percent. Since then, America has suffered two significant negative consequences:

1. The national debt has risen at a significant rate.
2. The net worth of the wealthiest individuals in our country has risen at a rapid rate.

OUR NATIONAL DEBT KEEPS PILING UP

Significantly lower tax rates for high-income individuals have transformed our country. Our government no longer collects enough revenue to operate without borrowing large sums daily. As a result, America's debt has surpassed its GDP, reaching about $39 trillion at the start of 2026, while the entire country produced $31.2 trillion in 2025.

These are staggering numbers. But math is math: $39 trillion in debt exceeds $30 trillion in income. Borrowing more than we earn isn't inherently the problem—individuals do it all the time, buying homes worth more than their annual income. The real issue is the trend. Imagine someone buying a home twice their yearly income, then borrowing more each year—whether their income rose or fell. Regardless of how well that person managed their debt, eventually banks and credit card companies would stop lending them more money.

As debt grows, servicing it consumes more of our tax revenue. Instead of investing in infrastructure like electrical grids or replacing dangerous, century-old bridges, we must divert funds to pay interest on our massive national debt.

Interestingly, those who accumulate debt fastest—Conservatives—continue to get elected. Republican presidential candidates often emphasize concerns about public debt and deficits, yet, over the past century, every Republican administration has increased the federal budget deficit by the time they left office. As discussed, larger deficits mean more borrowing, fueling a cycle that's hard to break.

THE TOP TAX RATES WERE HIGH AFTER THE GREAT DEPRESSION FOR A REASON

The Great Depression exposed many problems with our economy and our society. As discussed previously, Franklin D. Roosevelt implemented a wide range of government programs to solve many of those problems. He created the Federal Deposit Insurance Corporation (FDIC) to keep bankers honest and protect depositors. He created job programs to accomplish what the nation needed, like building airports and highways, while boosting the economy. He created Social Security to protect the elderly. Those who have worked their entire lives should not be homeless when they get too old to work. In addition to all that, he raised top tax rates to very high levels relative to where they had been before the Great Depression. Higher tax rates served several purposes:

- Disincentivize the concentration of wealth
- Incentivize workers sharing in the success of companies
- Keep more money in circulation
- Leave less money available for wild financial speculation

These programs and tax rates increased the number of middle-income citizens. When employees increased productivity for their employers, the tax structure kept the new profits from simply rising to the top and being skimmed off by their owners and top management. Companies could certainly retain all the money they need to run and expand their businesses, but it no longer made sense to pay top management and ownership an outsized amount of the money earned from increased productivity.

As for taxation, employees taking home more money led to a rapid increase in tax revenue. The government accumulated less debt because higher income for middle-income workers led to higher tax revenue.

When money concentrates in the hands of wealthy people, it costs everyone. The country gets less tax revenue. The velocity of the money —the rate at which it moves into the economy—slows down, to a crawl in some cases. When people earn so much money that extra income makes no difference in their lifestyles, they simply stockpile it.

And then the wealthy come up with schemes to avoid paying taxes on that money. Those schemes allow them to pay even less in taxes than middle-income taxpayers. For instance, CEOs receive some of their income in stock options. The value of those stock options determines their income. But until they exercise those options, meaning sell them or convert them to stock, they pay no taxes.

To increase their income, CEOs make corporate decisions to increase the value of the company's stock. Some of those decisions have nothing to do with innovation (offering new products or services.) Borrowing money to buy back shares of the company's stock, a practice that was illegal until 1982, increases the value of outstanding shares. That in turn increases the value of the CEO's stock options. When the CEO's stock options increase in value, the CEO's income increases. Except he does not simply take the additional income. He can borrow money against those options to support his lifestyle. Using that scheme, he pays no additional taxes. CEOs come up with these schemes because the concentration of wealth is an addiction.

All of that is legal though. The problem for the greater society is that we have yet to see these high-income citizens pay a fair share of their new income in taxes. When we get new income through raises or overtime, we do not get that choice. Causing the company to borrow money to buy back stock does not cost a CEO a dime in taxes. The increase in the value of his stock options does not cost him anything in taxes either. Borrowing against the value of his stock options costs him nothing in taxes. Good for him—right?

Tax dodging income benefits very high-income earners. It works less well for average-income earners. I can borrow money against the value of my home, and yes, I get a tax break on the interest. However, when the value of my home increases, I must pay taxes on the increase. Those taxes on the appreciation of my primary asset, my home, are called property taxes. The CEO does not have to pay taxes on the increased value of his major asset, his stock options, or his stock. That difference allows the CEO to access millions in income without ever paying income taxes. And for some billionaires, that is almost a way of life.

ECONOMIC ADVANTAGES CREATE A FEEDBACK LOOP

I get penalized for my home's increased value. The CEO is rewarded for the increase in the value of his stock options. How can we reconcile the obvious differences in the tax treatment of wealthy individuals with the tax treatment of middle-income individuals? It is called the IRS Code, and Congress controls what goes into the IRS Code.

In our recent political campaigning environment, we experienced one pivotal Supreme Court decision that allows tax policy disparities to continue. That decision is called Citizens United. The Supreme Court handed down its decision on the lawsuit Citizens United v. the Federal Election Commission in 2010.[i] The case overturned an earlier decision, Austin v. Michigan Chamber of Commerce.

In short, this decision gave corporations the right to spend unlimited sums on political campaigns. That decision has allowed some companies to spend millions or hundreds of millions to advocate for or against specific candidates or issues. This causes candidates to seek the approval of large companies on legislation. Candidates now know that those corporations will support them with favorable advertising come election time.

Case in point: Investment bankers get favorable tax treatment on profits made from relatively short-term deals. I call them "deals" because, in many cases, the investment bankers do not put any of their own money at risk. They simply coordinate investors and leverage to create financial transactions.

When middle-income people complete a real estate sale of a house, having never lived in that house, and take profits from the sale of that house, they pay taxes on those profits as ordinary income. But when investment bankers receive payouts from much larger transactions—in many cases having never even put money at risk—their cut of the profits or the growth in the value of those entities is taxed at a capital gains rate of 20 percent. This favorable income tax treatment is called carried interest.

Most Democratic and Republican politicians have acknowledged that this tax treatment is unfair. Barack Obama campaigned on eliminating the carried interest loophole, and so did Hillary Clinton, Donald Trump, and Joe Biden. All of the following pieces of legislation contained language to eliminate carried interest:

- Dodd-Frank (2010)
- Tax Cuts and Jobs Act (2017)
- Build Back Better Act (2021)
- Inflation Reduction Act (2022)

In every case, the power of millions in corporate campaign money influenced members of Congress to ensure one thing: Congressmen removed any language eliminating carried interest from the pending legislation. The power of corporations, because of the millions and millions they can pour into campaigns, ended up winning. The considerations of the people—especially considerations about reducing our national debt—end up losing.

The longer provisions like carried interest survive, the more wealth of high-value individuals and corporations concentrates. The more affluent they become, the less likely that congresspeople will vote against their preferences. The longer wealth concentration goes on, the more powerful they become. It's an endless cycle.

THE BENEFICIARIES OF TAX CUTS HOARD MONEY

Once Conservatives cut their tax burdens, billionaires gain the ability to grow wealth more easily. Since 1981, the top 5 percent of income earners have increased their net worth by trillions of dollars. They accomplished the feat by cutting costs and hoarding cash.

Employees are a major cost for businesses. This list shows some of the employee-related costs that can be cut:

- Head count
- Pay
- Pensions
- Health benefits
- Vacation and other leave
- Automation

CONSERVATIVES BUST UNIONS

Before Ronald Reagan, many workers in labor belonged to unions. Unions entered into contracts with employers, establishing important compensation factors captured in the list above. In addition, contracts dealt with hiring and firing practices, worker safety, hours, overtime, and other employee-related issues.

Then, around the time Reagan signed his massive tax cut, the Professional Air Traffic Controllers Organization (PATCO), a union for air traffic controllers, went on strike. Outdated equipment, understaffing, and chronic overtime prompted PATCO members to strike against their employer, the federal government. Reagan responded harshly, replacing thirteen thousand controllers and decertifying their union.

From that point forward, Conservatives spoke negatively about unions. They accused unions of spending their members' money to elect candidates that were Liberals. Consequently, from 1983 to 2025, union representation of employees declined from 20.1 percent down to just above 9.9 percent. The number of union-represented employees fell by 3.4 million during that period.

I remember that in my Detroit neighborhood, it seemed like everyone belonged to a union. Most of my neighbors belonged to the United Auto Workers, the UAW. I lived in a Black middle-income neighborhood. As I said, my next-door neighbor worked in a Cadillac assembly plant. He also drove a Cadillac. Back then, employees of automakers who worked on assembly lines made enough money to afford the cars they built. In fact, they took pride in buying the cars they built. They did not want to drive cars from competing brands into their plants' parking lots. Back then, when I drove past a manufacturing plant, I saw a parking lot filled with that manufacturer's cars.

More recently, when I drove past a BMW assembly plant in Alabama, I did not see many BMWs. In fact, I did not see many new cars of any brand. Manufacturers capitalized on lower labor costs by moving manufacturing from heavily unionized states, like Michigan, to so-called right-to-work states, like Alabama.

That practice started decades ago. It started with labor. But, in the intervening years, it has progressed through lower management and middle management. It seems that no one makes a decent wage but upper management.

COMPANIES OFFSHORE JOBS

My son, coincidentally, worked for a software company that developed software for auto dealerships. He worked there for nearly seven years. When he started, most of his team worked in the United States, but a small part of his team worked in India. Labor costs for software development and maintenance in India are substantially lower than costs in the United States.

In 2024, he got laid off. Over those seven years, his company slowly moved more of its development and testing offshore. His former company gradually reduced labor costs by continually shifting jobs from American workers to offshore workers. They went through several rounds of laying off American workers over the years. Finally, as 2025 approached, they informed my son that his tenure at the company would end at the end of 2024.

Some might say that this practice represents normal business efforts to increase returns to investors by lowering costs. That makes sense on a case-by-case basis. But when we look at the whole economy, the high-income investor segment of America has gained a larger share of the country's total wealth since 1983 by using these practices without the responsibility of the corresponding tax burden.

TODAY'S ECONOMY FORESHADOWS A SIGNIFICANT ECONOMIC CORRECTION

By 2025, the wealthiest 0.5 percent of the country, who held the highest share of wealth during the lead-up to the Great Depression, owned a larger share of the country's total wealth than the top 0.5 percent did in the 1920s. That is a bad sign.

When the Great Depression hit, America had imposed tariffs on the rest of the world. Herbert Hoover signed the Smoot-Hawley Tariff Act into law on June 30, 1930. By the time Franklin D. Roosevelt took office in 1933, the unemployment rate had risen to about 25 percent, the stock market had crashed, and many banks had failed. And when I say that banks had failed, I mean that depositors could not retrieve the money they had previously deposited.

To prevent the American people from losing their deposits, the federal government created the FDIC. That entity assesses bank soundness based on its cash reserves, loan portfolio, investment portfolio, and other factors. The FDIC exists to monitor banks to protect depositors against the natural greed and inordinate risk-taking into which banks tend to venture.

Risk-taking was not the only factor that helped bring about the Great Depression. Hoarding wealth created the environment for that massive risk-taking. To tamp down the concentration of wealth, the federal government enacted a tax bracket of 79 percent for income earners who earned over $5 million a year.

Let me explain something about taxation. The federal government did not tax all the income of those making over $5 million a year at 79 percent. They taxed each level of income the same for every taxpayer. In 1935, the federal tax system had thirty-three separate tax brackets. For instance, $0 to $4,000 was taxed at 4 percent. So, no matter how much total money someone made, the first $4,000 was taxed at 4 percent. At each level of income, the tax rate increased. After the first thirty-two brackets, the income over $5,000,000 would be taxed at 79 percent. If a person made $6 million in income, the government would tax only that last $1 million at 79 percent.

Conservatives often give us the impression that the federal government would tax the entire personal income of a wealthy person at the top tax bracket. They might ask the question: "Is it fair that my income should be taxed at 79 percent because I'm successful?" If they put that question to us, everyone would answer: "No." But, as I've just explained, tax brackets don't work like that.

During the Great Depression, as always, the federal government needed revenue. But above that, the government wanted to discourage individuals from gathering massive amounts of wealth. If business owners or upper-level managers of large corporations decided that they wanted to pay themselves $50 million in a year, the federal government would tax the last $45 million at 79 percent. The effect of a high tax rate was to discourage wealth hoarding.

Today, we have the same problem the country was experiencing in 1932: Individuals gather massive amounts of wealth. Since Reagan, the highest tax rate has hovered around 40 percent. Democrats raised the highest tax rate slightly, and Republicans lowered it, but it stays close to 40 percent. So, we have no disincentive to prevent ridiculous amounts of wealth from gathering in the hands of a few. Those analyzing the causes of the Great Depression discovered that people with large sums of money to invest faced specific financial problems.

Their insatiable thirst for more money causes wild speculation in the markets and the need to push the government for lower and lower tax burdens. If this continues, America is headed for the same cliff again.

WE SHOULDN'T HATE ON THOSE WHO MAKE A BUNCH OF MONEY

Fair taxation doesn't equate to hating those who acquire great wealth. Look at it this way: If a company eliminates two hundred employees from their payroll, they eliminate many costs. In many cases, the bulk of those savings goes straight to that company's bottom line. The company's profits increase. Their stock value might also increase.

Every time we witness one of these events, we should also realize a few things:

- Each employee contributes 14 percent of his entire salary in FICA taxes.
- People who make millions have a cap of $184,500 on the amount of their income subject to FICA taxes.
- Many of the people who profit from those layoffs will rarely pay federal taxes on their newfound profits.

So, in addition to putting additional people out of work, the federal government will see few of the tax dollars it would normally see from rank-and-file workers. In a country in so much debt, we can ill afford to incentivize any corporate employment changes that result in lower tax revenues.

This is just one of the many ways the concentration of wealth hurts our country. Until we have a full reckoning with these schemes, our country will keep inching toward financial ruin. At that point, depending on what's left of our government, we will be forced to make the changes we could voluntarily make right now.

CHAPTER 12
DEMOCRATS MUST MESSAGE

> *Americans primarily know Democrats by what Republicans say about them, because Republicans speak and write more about Democrats than Democrats speak and write about themselves."*

HUMILITY GETS DEMOCRATS ZERO POINTS

DEMOCRATS LOSE elections because most who read this will have never seen comparisons between Republican and Democratic economic results. Democrats have a credible record of economic growth and stability. The numbers speak for themselves, and the numbers do not lie. Job growth, GDP growth, and growth in the value of stocks all prove that the policies of Democratic administrations lead to economies that work better than those of Republicans. And economic growth helps all citizens.

Democrats assume that all Americans know them by their work, but Americans primarily know Democrats by what Republicans say about them, because Republicans speak and write more about Democrats than Democrats speak and write about themselves. Republicans write fictitious accounts of what Democrats have done, and Democrats do not speak enough about what they themselves do.

Democrats must speak more about their accomplishments, but they must also get the message out first and then keep their accomplishments in the public eye, even when they are not in power.

Like most productive people, Democrats do not go around bragging about the work they have done and the successes they have experienced. They concern themselves with solving the next problem and planning for the one after that. We will not see a staged cabinet meeting with a Democratic president's cabinet secretaries praising him on camera on cue, one after the other. Democrats will not put on the shows like those of Donald Trump and his cabinet members. That would be like a farmer standing in the town square telling all his neighbors how he plowed his fields, fertilized, and planted. Farmers do not have time for that. They spend their time executing the plans they made three days prior, planning for the next three days, and thinking about the coming harvest.

NO PARTY CAN WIN WITHOUT EFFECTIVE MESSAGING

In the current environment, messaging is not a luxury. Messaging helps voters understand the difference between a party that has a history of destroying the economy (Republicans) and one that has a history of producing and sustaining great economies (Democrats).

Messaging focused on history gives Democrats an obvious advantage. Since Democrats have delivered great economies over the last century, Democrats have unmatched receipts. They must use that longstanding record. They must direct the voting public's minds toward their successful history. To direct the pubic, candidates must know the history themselves.

If voters hear both Republicans and Democrats talk about the great economies they plan to create, they hear two parties attempting to predict the future. No one can effectively predict the future.

However, when Democrats talk about their great track record of economic growth, reducing deficits, efficient government spending, and recession-free economies, Republicans must lie to match that. When they force Republicans into that arena, Democrats create an opportunity to expose Republicans. Also, in that arena, Democrats can give all citizens hope. Hope is a great feeling. People always remember how we make them feel, remember? Democrats will create this feeling based on a track record. Republicans cannot do that.

To be an effective political party, Democrats must message regularly and effectively. Even if Republicans did not participate in full-scale deception and outright lying, they have no responsibility to laud the successes of Democratic policies. So, because of the way competitive politics work, Democrats must step up and trumpet their success.

Democrats also need to point out, with great regularity and candor, the failures of Republicans. As much as highlighting Democrats' successes and their opponent's failures might not be a natural task for productive people, it's necessary for Democrats as a political party. The voting public needs to have a clearer picture of their voting options.

THE PUBLIC DOES NOT KNOW

As an experiment, I started testing a single statistic among my closest relatives and acquaintances. I asked those I knew were politically active the following question:

Who was the last Republican president to leave office with a lower deficit than when he entered office?

It's a simple question. It should not be a challenge for politically active Democrats. Why? Because every Democratic presidential campaign should have shouted the answer to that question from the rooftops for at least the last fifty or sixty years. Every Democratic candidate running for Congress should have put that fact on a repeated loop as a regular part of their campaign messaging.

I'm not just saying that because I want Democrats to win. I'm saying that because the country should have this information to help it make informed decisions about which party to choose to run America's economy.

I've also asked this same question of Republicans. But none of them knew the answer either.

> ***Question 1:*** *Who was the last Conservative (Republican) president to leave office with a lower federal budget deficit than when he entered office?*
> ***Answer:*** *Calvin Coolidge in 1929.*

Conservatives' economics have not reduced the speed at which we pile up debt in America since the Great Depression. Since then, every single Republican presidential administration has left office with a larger federal budget deficit than when they entered office.

But what about employment? Surely the economics of Conservatives helped that situation. Wrong again.

> ***Question 2:*** *Who were recent presidents to leave office with an unemployment rate of less than 5 percent?*
> ***Answer:***
> *Joe Biden (Democrat, 2025) with an unemployment rate of 4.0 percent*
> *Barack Obama (Democrat, 2017) with an unemployment rate of 4.7 percent*
> *Bill Clinton (Democrat, 2001) with an unemployment rate of 4.2 percent*

> ***Question 3:*** *Who was the last Republican president to leave office with an unemployment rate less than 5 percent since the Great Depression?*
> ***Answer:*** *No one*

BAD OR INADEQUATE MESSAGING HURTS EVERYONE

Again, most did not know the answers to these questions because Democrats stink at messaging. And some might say, "That's why they lose" (like I said earlier). But the lack of messaging hurts more than just Democratic candidates. It hurts all Americans.

If Americans choose a Republican president, they unknowingly choose the candidate of a party that will guarantee a worse economy, more borrowing, and more spending. Results of Republican presidents since the Great Depression, nearly one hundred years, have taught us that. When Democrats do not message properly, they fail in their responsibility as a party to inform the American voting public about both the Democratic and Republican choices.

Some might say, "This is politics, and it does not affect me. Whoever wins wins. I'll just go about my life. Please cut the noise off." But sometimes, the choices we make or allow others to make for us on Election Day affect us in undeniable ways.

Take farmers in Iowa. In 2024, 70 percent of Iowa farmers who voted did so for Donald Trump, but some did not vote at all. Whether farmers voted in the 2024 election or not, many Iowa farmers suffered the negative effects of Trump's policies.

Between January and November 2025, unemployment in America rose from 4.0 percent to 4.6 percent. That's an increase of 15 percent in the number of Americans out of work. America ended 2025 with job growth of 181 thousand. In contrast, in 2024, under Joe Biden, the economy had added 2.2 million jobs.

Private-sector jobs took a hit, and we expect that unemployment will remain on an upward trajectory.

This means the following:

- Many of the people who voted for Donald Trump will lose their jobs.
- Many of the people who voted against Trump will lose their jobs.
- Many of the people who did not vote at all will lose their jobs.

Many Iowa farmers lost their farms in 2026, and several of them have gone bankrupt. Among those who went bankrupt, several have committed suicide.

Some Democratic candidates knew the history of Republican economics, as those Democrats were running during the last election cycle. Democrats failed to adequately inform the electorate that voting for Trump would mean higher unemployment based on an almost one-hundred-year record. Democrats did the voting public a grave disservice.

Democrats knew about the irresponsible fiscal policies of Republicans. They knew that Republicans campaign on one thing and then do, in many cases, another. Since their messaging failed to make those facts known to the electorate, Democrats failed the country. The electorate may have thought that they could rely on either candidate to sustain a good economy, including stable GDP growth and low unemployment.

HOW CAN DEMOCRATS CHANGE THIS?

Democrats must separate themselves from the mire of Republican politics. To do that, Democrats must distinguish themselves, in the public's mind, from Republicans' low, immoral, dishonest speech and elevate themselves in a way that proves their integrity. The custom of comity, civility, and face-saving with respect to opponents has no place in today's political arena.

But calling a liar a liar does not make them uncivil; it makes them more trustworthy. No lie told by Conservatives about Democrats should go undeclared. And I do mean to say "undeclared," not "unchallenged." When they declare a lie, they do not have to challenge it. If a liar wants to prove his lie to be the truth (he cannot, by the way), he can always attempt to do so. But wasting time on a debate stage proving that a pathological liar has lied is futile. To a liar, the supply of possible lies is infinite.

However, liars do not like to be called out on their lies, so they will push back. Democrats must push forward every time Republican opponents push back. If the liar reasserts his lie, Democrats must reassert that he is lying. If he offers illegitimate proof, Democrats must reassert that he is lying. After all, a half-truth is a full lie.

Liars do not give up on asserting lies after one or two attempts. Candidates must prepare to rebuff lies four or five or even six times each. The listening public must know that Republicans have lied. Often, that means the process looks like the following:

- Call them on their lie.
- They offer an unsubstantiated basis for their assertions.
- Call them on the lie again.
- They stand behind their invalid proof.
- Call them on the lie again.
- Rinse and repeat.

Candidates can never let up. They can never let the lie walk. They can never allow proof that contains no substance to go unchallenged. Ever.

Candidates must also always stand prepared. The best tool of deception is surprise. When we rebut one lie, we must be prepared for another, and another, and another. Don't allow a single lie to go unnoticed.

In the 2012 Republican presidential primary, Mitt Romney won the Republican presidential nomination. Romney picked Paul Ryan as his running mate. Ryan and Joe Biden (at the time, the sitting vice president) had an exchange about tax cuts.

Biden's debate against Ryan is a classic example of not letting a lie walk. This exchange is a great example of a Democrat executing on the principle of not letting a falsehood continue, no matter how many times the opponent presented the lie:

Paul Ryan: You can cut tax rates by 20 percent and still preserve important preferences for the middle class... [False premise]
Joe Biden: Not mathematically possible. [Callout #1]
Paul Ryan: It is mathematically possible. It's been done before. It's precisely what we are proposing. [Reassertion of false premise]
Joe Biden: It has never been done before. [Callout #2]
Paul Ryan: It has been done a couple of times. [Unsubstantiated reassertion]
Joe Biden: It has never been done before. [Callout #3]
Paul Ryan: Jack Kennedy lowered tax rates, increased growth. Ronald Reagan...
Joe Biden: Oh, now you are Jack Kennedy.

Paul Ryan: Republicans and Democrats have worked together on this.
Joe Biden: But we told each other what we were going to do. When we did it with Reagan, he said: "Here are the things we are going to cut." That's what he said...[i]

After this exchange, they moved on to another topic.

I want to make a few points about the substance of this exchange. Republicans proposed a 20 percent tax cut to corporations and middle-income citizens during the 2012 campaign. Biden called them out on their lack of detail. They showed no way of paying for such a huge tax cut. Ryan believed, as Republicans since Ronald Reagan have believed, that tax cuts pay for themselves through economic growth, which then creates more tax revenue.

Biden made the point that tax cuts have never paid for themselves through growth. Biden spoke the truth. Ryan tried to reassure the audience that tax cuts pay for themselves. Biden makes definitive statements: "Not mathematically possible" and "It has never been done before."

Biden called out the lie. He directly contradicted Ryan's statement. That left Ryan to go back to forty years, then twenty years, and then give up the argument. Why? Because the most recent example of tax cuts not paying for themselves was George W. Bush, only four years before.

Although the example of Kennedy's tax cut was somewhat valid, in that he cut taxes and grew the economy, Kennedy cut the tax rate to less than 8 percent for top income earners, those making over $2,900,000 a year in 2025 dollars.

Using Reagan as an example does not make sense. Reagan cut the top tax rate by 60 percent and grew the national debt by a record that no subsequent administration has rivaled: about 187 percent. During the Reagan administration, the United States moved from a lender nation to a debtor nation. We have yet to return to our former lender status. As of the second quarter of 2026, America's debt has exceeded $39 trillion.

Now, it might seem harsh to call what Paul Ryan asserted in that debate a lie. But there are a few ways someone can tell a lie:

1. They can assert something as a fact that they know to be false.
2. They can assert something as a fact that they do not know to be true.
3. They can assert something as a fact that is only true out of context. This is otherwise known as a half-truth.

Perhaps there are more ways to lie, but I'm familiar with these three.

Since Ryan is a leader in the Republican Party, he should know more about the history of Republican economic policy and its results. If he does, then his comments were a lie using technique #1.

If, as a leader of his party, he asserted that growth would pay for large tax cuts and he was ignorant of the fact that it has never happened, he was telling a lie using technique #2. It could be a half-truth, but nothing in what he said is true.

So, either his overall claim that they did not want to rack up larger deficits and debt was false, or his claim that they could give 20 percent tax cuts and still pay for other programs without increasing the deficit was false. But he was lying when he asserted that both 20 percent tax cuts and moving toward a balanced budget could happen.

CALLING LIARS OUT REQUIRES KNOWLEDGE

Joe Biden, at the time of the debate, had a long history in the Senate. Biden, before he became vice president, had served in the Senate for thirty years. Biden had experienced a long list of Democratic accomplishments and disappointments. Not many people have that much detailed information about the workings of our government. In his case, his experiences date back to Richard Nixon's second term.

That's where policy teams come in. Democrats must establish messaging that includes the party's history of success. They must also teach their candidates the history of that success. Then Democratic candidates must run their campaigns using Democratic history to create comfort in the minds of voters that Democrats will stabilize and grow the economy as they have in the past.

Just as importantly, Democratic candidates must use that same knowledge to preach against the failures of Republicans. They must point out all the recessions that have taken place during Republican presidencies. They must make comparisons between the growth of the economy during Democratic administrations and the decline during Republican administrations.

As they execute on these important public information campaigns, Democratic candidates must also combat incessant lying. That's the hard part. Liars want the conversation to degrade into a conversation about who is lying. The goal is to keep the opponent on equal footing with them.

Here are a few strategies to combat that technique:

- Never ask questions. Only make statements. A question is just another opportunity for a liar to lie.
- Tell the truth. Always. Just because some liars get away with lying does not mean that everyone will. Integrity and trust mean we can never resort to that. Voters want people they can trust.
- Ask a question, but also answer it. For example: "Who increased the national debt by the greatest percentage during his presidency? Ronald Reagan by 187 percent."
- Always blame the president. Never allow opponents to blame Congress. There is one person in Washington responsible for allowing Congress to spend money, and that is the president of the United States. He must sign every spending bill. Whether to sign each bill is up to him and only him. The responsibility rests on his shoulders. Congress rarely overrides spending bills.

These techniques help us to minimize the effects of a lying opponent. But the most effective way to silence lies is with the truth. That technique requires knowledge. When we have knowledge, we can handle an onslaught of lies.

Next, and finally, expect lies. Because we know performance statistics, we can call out lies. But remember, all we have to do is call a lie a lie. Unless prompted, we have no need to prove that a person is lying. Let them try to prove they are telling the truth. The person who asserts something as fact has the responsibility to prove the fact. When they can't, they will tell more lies. We can then call them out on those new lies. Eventually, we will be asked to explain the truth, and at that point, we can show how they are lying. When that happens, the truth will have better contrast and effectiveness against the lies.

Now, that said, I'm not a messaging expert. But I do know how to deal with liars. I'm sure experts have more sophisticated techniques, but do not miss the point. Democrats have a serious responsibility to the electorate to properly inform them. If they cannot handle opponents who lie, they will continue to subject American citizens to economies that fail by losing elections.

Democrats must message effectively, or America will never force Republicans to become an effective party.

CHAPTER 13
STEPS TOWARD BETTER CHOICES

> *When we recognize anxiety-inducing language and actions, we should call [it] out to our peers....Just as whisper campaigns spread negative information, informed voters talking to other voters can spread warnings and good information."*

I HAVE FOCUSED ON ECONOMIC, psychological, and social factors that influence Conservatives and lead them to vote in elections. When Conservatives implement White Anxiety, we have seen how it can negatively affect elections and produce administrations that win using such deception.

In this chapter, I want to discuss effective steps to help us make better choices. We will focus on the following:

- How to evaluate economic policy
- How to evaluate political rhetoric
- How to diversify information sources
- How to recognize qualified candidates

STOP VOTING FOR ANY REPUBLICAN WHO STILL BELIEVES IN SUPPLY-SIDE ECONOMICS

Supply-side economics has plagued the U.S. economy since the early 1980s. Using the name "supply-side" seems to sanitize the actual result of that philosophy in economics. You could just call it the grift of corporations and wealthy individuals..

We provided support for companies in the form of tax cuts when economic growth turned negative. Think about that. The government attempted to fix the economy by giving companies access to more money to help the economy. I'm not an economist, but I do know what people do when they receive money—lots of money—that they did not earn and do not need to live. They do not appreciate it, and they feel entitled to more.

If people wonder why that does not make sense, I'm going to give a very short lesson on our economy. Seventy percent of America's GDP comes from consumer spending.[i] Giving money to companies when GDP growth slows, on the off chance they will create jobs, makes no sense. We know that providing more opportunities to consumers will always create jobs. Why? Because, in economics, the income of middle-income and lower-income individuals has a higher velocity. That means money in the hands of wealthy people moves slowly, while money in the hands of middle- and lower-income households moves into the economy much faster.

The other thing we know is that when Ronald Reagan gave tax breaks to wealthy Americans—or almost anyone else—it did not cause enough growth to make up for the cost of the tax breaks. That's one of the fallacies of supply-side economics. It does not work. It has never worked. Since we first tried that theory, it has caused our country to accumulate more debt.

HOW DO WE IDENTIFY SUPPLY-SIDERS?

We might never hear the term "supply-side economics" from a single candidate. What we will hear is "tax cuts." Let's think about that for a minute. As of the second quarter of 2026, America has a standing debt of $39 trillion. Our federal government funds its operations through tax revenue. Since Ronald Reagan took office in 1981, we have struggled to collect enough tax revenue to run the country. When we do not raise enough in tax revenue to run the country, we call that a deficit. And yet some of us would vote for candidates who promise to reduce the possibility of more revenue by giving tax cuts. Having massive debt and voting for someone who is guaranteed to make that debt larger got us where we are today. We have to reverse that trend.

Running a temporary deficit in bad times happens. My air conditioner breaks, and I must spend more money that month than I earned. That's a deficit. I can do that for a month or two. But if I do that every month, I will go broke. We can all understand that.

The same is true for America. Borrowing money during an emergency makes sense. We would rather take that money from savings, but we already have a huge debt, so that's not possible. Because of tax cuts, America borrows money when times are good, and in most cases, that borrowing isn't for investments but just to run the government.

We cannot borrow money in good times and bad times and expect to remain solvent. We must denounce that as idiocy. We should not expect that giving tax breaks to the wealthiest in our country—or anyone else, for that matter—will do anything other than what it has done for the last forty-plus years: drive us into recession.

Look for the person who promises massive tax cuts, then run in the other direction. Find another candidate. Find one who wants America to collect enough tax revenue to pay for what we budget as a country. We have not done that since Bill Clinton was president, twenty-five years ago. Let's elect candidates who promise to increase revenue, not cut it. Keep voting for people who campaign on sound fiscal policy until we balance the federal budget.

WE MUST PREPARE OURSELVES FOR WHITE ANXIETY

Con artists cannot successfully practice their craft when their prospective victims suspect them. When we know how to identify the con, we will stop falling victim to it.

First, we must recognize people attempting to induce anxiety in us about others. When I say "others," I mean non-Whites and immigrants. Candidates show their hand with a few easy-to-spot traits:

- They talk way too much about other people. They talk very little about what they are doing or plan to do.
- They blame important events, problems, and challenges on other people.
- They have the support of overtly racist groups, causes, and tactics. They receive that support without ever pushing back.
- They take no responsibility for the failings of the government. When government systems like FEMA fail, they offer no solutions, no apologies, and no changes. They also blame previous administrations for those problems.
- They blame without proof. When entirely new systems are created that solve no discernible problems, that should trouble us.
- They lie. When candidates are caught in lies they cannot reconcile, that should alert us all. Candidates who will not apologize for mistakes should fire off our alerts.

Next, when we recognize anxiety-inducing language and actions, we should call them out to our peers. Call them out on social media. For those with large platforms, we should call them out there. Just as whisper campaigns spread negative information, informed voters talking to other voters can spread warnings and good information. Candidates will get the message and stop, or they will lose. If they do not get the message, we will help prevent them from gaining elective office or being reelected.

After we call these things out, we should reject them. We can talk to our friends and neighbors. That's important. We can also reject these things by refusing to vote for anyone who practices this deception. When candidates try to get us to vote against someone based on feelings and perceptions, they are engaging in a ploy. They should always work to convince us of their worthiness by selling themselves. They should not simply try to get us to vote against someone else or another party. We should always ask ourselves what each candidate brings to the table. "Why should I give them my precious vote?" should always be the question on our minds.

Yes, campaigning is a competition. And yes, competitors do compare themselves to each other. That's a natural part of the campaign process. But when most of the campaign becomes about voting against a candidate's opponent, that's when suspicion should swell within us.

In addition, candidates who campaign on destroying more than they build should also raise suspicion. America has great challenges. We need help with those challenges substantially more than we need to destroy existing programs.

Speak against these things during open forums as well. If candidates have public meetings, we should ask questions focusing on what they plan to accomplish should we vote for them. If most of their answers involve tearing down, and a minor part of their answers involve strategies to build up, then reject them.

DIVERSIFY NEWS MEDIA CHOICES

We should never trust any single news source for all our news. If we trust any single source, that source could collude with anxiety-inducing candidates to help groom us into voting for or against a specific party. Watch and listen to a variety of news sources. News sources should not serve as pundits; they should report the news. C-SPAN serves as a news channel by reporting the proceedings of Congress, and also has a morning call-in show where they invite politicians from both parties.

All news sources should bring back the fairness doctrine. The fairness doctrine required news organizations to present multiple viewpoints on issues like political policy and opinion. It went into effect in 1949 and remained an FCC rule until the Reagan administration.

The great thing about this rule was that whatever political candidates and pundits said had to be thoroughly explored. This made misinformation less likely. Any misinformation by one side was quickly corrected by the other side. So, opponents called out lying before we ever thought it was a fact. Deception cannot survive in that environment.

Since Republicans and their pundits like Sean Hannity and Rush Limbaugh branded all broadcast media as liberal media, many Conservatives now distrust major broadcast media. It's time to take an objective look at all media again. If, after we do this, we discover that Hannity, Limbaugh, and others were correct, so be it. But writing mainstream media off as potential news sources only causes the media of Conservatives to have an outsized influence in information gathering for their viewers. They will miss important information necessary for objective decision-making about issues and candidates. Again, this puts their viewers at risk of being groomed by Republican candidates.

If news stations of any stripe believe that we have no other source of news, they will tend to believe they can steer our thinking about political issues however they wish. In some ways, they become operatives in politicians' and parties' efforts to move voter opinion in one direction or another.

We want to make sure that news organizations report the news. Their job should be to chronicle facts, including facts that might not sit well with their viewers. Their ability to omit facts that make us uncomfortable or to over-report certain kinds of news runs counter to our interests as citizens.

Do not forget that freedom of the press, established in the First Amendment, protects the press from government interference. But it does not protect us from the press, from other companies, or from ownership influencing the information they report. Our disdain for dishonest reporting and our requirement to hear all sides of an issue demand our attention. We must make sure that press outlets hear from us when they get off track.

VOTE FOR QUALIFIED CANDIDATES

It turns out that people who work to lower the federal budget deficit by raising revenue fare better in the economy. They have fewer recessions and leave office with lower deficits. So, if someone campaigns any time soon on cutting taxes when America's government has not taken in enough tax money to run itself since Bill Clinton left office in 2001, they insult our intelligence. They want to consign us to borrowing money every day for the rest of our lives and the lives of our children and grandchildren. That candidate signals to us that they are not qualified for the job.

Candidates who have shown themselves to be untrustworthy are not qualified to lead our country. Liars do not make good leaders. Convicted criminals do not make good leaders. Those who would cheat on their spouses do not make good leaders. If the person who sleeps in the bed next to a man cannot trust him, neither can we as voters. Those who engage in other activities that demonstrate low moral character disqualify themselves as candidates seeking positions of trust in the leadership of our country.

In times of crisis, our leaders must possess the integrity to look Americans in the eye and demand great efforts to help bring the country through bad times. An untrustworthy person cannot do that.

Morally bad candidates do not turn good after they win. They end up dragging our country into their immoral activities. Thus, it's important to do the following:

- Make morality part of every candidate's decision.
- Make sure that candidates have a plan to manage the economy.
- Make sure that candidates plan to do constructive work with the presidency.
- Do not consider destructive candidates qualified for your vote.

If we stop allowing unqualified candidates to get our votes, they will stop running. The president, governor, county supervisor, mayor, and city council member should all be people our children can look up to. We should vote *for* people, not against them. And when people perform well, we should vote to reelect them. If they do poorly, we should vote them out. We should vote "Thank you" and "I hate you" when warranted—but with our heads, not our hearts.

We should not ignore elections when times are good. If we do, we have a pretty good chance of allowing a person to rise to office who will cause the economy to transition from a good economy to a bad economy.

American citizens do not get to turn away. We do not get to stop paying attention. We do not get to phone it in. Since we are the most important part of our democracy, we have a job to do in every election. That includes every special election and every local election. If we stop paying attention, be assured that the unqualified and the dishonest will take over. Then we will have allowed a mess that we could have prevented if we had just paid attention.

BIG REPUTATION AND A BIG RESPONSIBILITY

Just because someone becomes president does not mean they care about our country. They might care more about themselves than our country. Voters hold the keys to the White House. We stand guard to prevent anyone who has not proven to us their worthiness to lead this great country.

Just because a person belongs to the party we identify with does not mean we must lend them our personal endorsement by voting for them. What are we, members of a gang? We do not have to conform. We have individual private voting stalls for that very reason. We shouldn't make a bad decision because of peer pressure.

But know this: if we degrade the qualifications of candidates, we will, in turn, degrade the progress of our country. America has always provided great leadership to the rest of the world. One famous quote says of America:

> *America is great because she is good. If America ceases to be good, America will cease to be great."*

We should take this observation to heart. We must realize that other countries and their citizens will not voluntarily follow our lead if we cease to be good. Once we step down from our leadership position in the world, we will cease to be great. If we open the leadership stage to others, we may never get it back.

We must guard our hearts from White Anxiety and vote for qualified candidates.

PROVIDE A SAFE SPACE FOR THOSE SHEDDING WHITE ANXIETY

Sometimes our fellow Americans seek an emotional connection with others. And, unfortunately, politicians take advantage of their need to connect. Some of the toxic communities that politicians set up to take advantage of those people eventually crumble under the weight of truth and reality.

I have attempted to show some of that reality in this book. Some will read this book and make important decisions about how to change their lives, and especially about how to vote. They might very well seek connection with some who heretofore had not shared their political ideologies.

Whatever we do, we should make those people feel safe. When they leave the embrace of their current communities, they need to have somewhere to go. Let that place be with those who want to build a better government through better electoral choices.

CHAPTER 14
CONCLUSION

> *America's Constitution establishes a government that enables the country to succeed. If run properly, our country can continue to progress and accomplish great things. We have a great structure."*

WE, as American citizens, have the ultimate power over who governs us. America is a representative democracy, otherwise known as a republic. Our votes put our representatives in office.

The writers of the Constitution made Congress—the representatives of the people—the most powerful branch of government, placing it first in the document as Article I.

Congress can oust the president. Congress can impeach and remove judges. Congress has oversight over the other branches of government and controls the government's financial resources. Neither of the other branches can spend a dime unless Congress appropriates the money.

That said, the power to elect representatives and the power to send them packing give us, the people, the ultimate sway over what our government does and does not do. The power to determine who represents us puts our index fingers on the eject button for every seat occupied by every person in government.

We should take that power seriously by observing a few rules:

- Take a sober-minded approach to electing representatives
- Seek to elect qualified candidates
- Stop voting simply based on labels
- Stay away from any candidate who espouses supply-side economics
- Vote based on the person, not the emotions the person provokes

America's Constitution establishes a government that enables the country to succeed. If we run our country properly, we can continue to progress and accomplish great things. We have a great structure. We have massive resources. We have great wealth.

We must guard these advantages, realizing that everything we possess as a country is delicate. Ronald Reagan once said, "Freedom is a fragile thing, and it's never more than one generation away from extinction. It is not ours by way of inheritance; it must be fought for and defended constantly by each generation, for it comes only once to a people. And those in world history who have known freedom and then lost it have never known it again."[i]

That idea must carry into every aspect of our well-being as a country. We must protect our solvency as a country. Massive amounts of debt also threaten our way of life. Electing a responsible president will do more to guard those resources than anything else we can do.

We must also work against the egregious concentration of wealth in our country. Remember the quote from Justice Louis Brandeis: "We can have democracy in this country, or we can have great wealth concentration in the hands of a few, but we cannot have both."[ii] Anyone who promotes supply-side economics promotes the concentration of wealth.

Finally, vote for candidates who have a plan. Don't vote for candidates who try to excite your emotions against their opponents. At the time of this writing, some feel that America is in a bad place. Our debt is out of control. We find ourselves in another armed conflict in the Middle East. We may be losing the support of our allies. Most of these problems stem from electing representatives and an administration that do not understand the value of our government.

Now is the time to reverse the trend of voting based on feelings and begin to vote based on competence and track record. Let's think more than we feel. Let's vote as if the survival of our country depends on it—because it does.

NOTES

PREFACE

i. National Bureau of Economic Research (NBER)
ii. Bureau of Labor Statistics (BLS)
iii. Martin Luther King Jr., "A Letter from Birmingham Jail," *Ebony* (August 1963): 23–32.

INTRODUCTION

i. U.C. Berkley Letters in Science, September 25, 2025 - https://ls.berkeley.edu/news/psychology-study-confirms-positive-emotions-fade-faster-negative-emo tions
ii. Keni Hines, A Global History of Blacks in the 19th Century: Detailed Chronologically from 1800 to 1899 (Armstrong Smith, 2021).
iii. Jeremy Diamond, "Trump: I Could 'Shoot Somebody and I Wouldn't Lose Voters,'" CNN, last updated January 24, 2016, https://www.cnn.com/2016/01/23/politics/donald-trump-shoot-somebody-support/.
iv. Amark Foundation, updated February 2023, "U.S. Presidents and the Federal Deficit",https://amarkfoundation.org/reports/u-s-presidents-and-the-federal-deficit/
v. National Bureau of Economic Research (NBER) - https://www.nber.org/research/business-cycle-dating
vi. The Bureau of Labor Statistics - bls.gov

1. WE NEED TWO PRODUCTIVE PARTIES

i. https://www.investopedia.com/financial-edge/0210/rules-that-warren-buffett-lives-by.aspx
ii. George H. W. Bush, campaign speech, April 10, 1980, Carnegie-Mellon University, Pittsburgh, Pennsylvania.
iii. John Maynard Keynes, *The General Theory of Employment, Interest and Money* (Palgrave Macmillan, 1936)
iv. National Bureau of Economic Research (NBER)
v. The Bureau of Labor Statistics - bls.gov
vi. 2 Thessalonians 3:10 (KJV).
vii. Bureau of Labor Statistics, Beyond the Numbers, "How does consumer spending change during boom, recession, and recovery?", June 2014, bls.gov
viii. *Major Factors in the Prediction of National Life Expectancy: GDP and Unemployment, United States Senate Committee on Environment and Public Works* (2011) (testimony of M. Harvey Brenner, professor).

ix. Irving Dilliard, ed., Mr. Justice Brandeis: Great American (Modern View Press, 1941), 42.
x. Samantha Ayoub, "Farm Bankruptcies Continued to Climb in 2025," American Farm Bureau Federation, February 9, 2026, https://www.fb.org/market-intel/farm-bankruptcies-continued-to-climb-in-2025.

2. WHAT ARE CONSERVATIVES?

i. I Timothy 3:1-13 (KJV)
ii. Grover Norquist, Morning Edition, National Public Radio, 2001
iii. Ronald Reagan, First Inaugural Address, January 20, 1981
iv. Eleanor Skelly et al., "Trump Says It's 'Not Possible' for the U.S. to Pay for Medicaid, Medicare and Day Care: 'We're Fighting Wars,'" NBC News, last updated April 2, 2026, https://www.nbcnews.com/politics/donald-trump/trump-says-not-possible-us-pay-medicaid-medicare-daycare-re-fighting-w-rcna266381.
v. The People of the State of New York v. Donald J. Trump, 2024 NY Slip Op 24328 (Sup. Ct., N.Y. County Dec. 16, 2024).
vi. E. Jean Carroll v. Donald J. Trump, No. 20-3977 (2d Cir. Apr. 21, 2023).
vii. Donald Trump, 2024 Presidential Debate, ABC, September 10, 2024
viii. Abraham Lincoln, *The Gettysburg Address*, Gettysburg, PA, November 19, 1863
ix. Ronald Reagan, Ronald Reagan Library, News Conference, Rosemont Ballroom, Chicago, IL, August 12, 1986

3. WHAT ARE LIBERALS?

i. United States Constitution, Article VI, Clause 2
ii. *With Honors*, directed by Alek Keshishian (Warner Bros. Pictures, 1994).
iii. Revelation 22:18–19.
iv. United States Constitution, Article V

4. HOW WHITE ANXIETY WORKS

i. NBC News, Latino voters in Florida react to Trump, July 2024
ii. May 31, 2024, October 6, 2024 - Campaign rally in Juneau, WI, October 31 on Tucker Carlson
iii. April 2, 2024, Green Bay, Wisconsin
iv. Presidential Debate between Trump and Harris on September 10, 2024
v. Morning Joe debunks Trump's crime rate claims - March 29, 2024
vi. White House Press conference on August 26, 2025
vii. Shreya Biswas, "US Job Growth Was Overstated by 1 Million in 2025 After Massive Revision, Biggest Cut in 20 Years - What It Means Now," *Economic Times*, last updated February 16, 2026, https://economictimes.indiatimes.com/news/international/us/us-job-growth-was-overstated-by-1-million-in-2025-after-massive-revision-biggest-cut-in-20-years-what-it-means-now/articleshow/128424208.cms.

viii. American Civil Liberties Union,"Smart Justice, Mass Incarceration" https://www.aclu.org/issues/smart-justice/mass-incarceration
ix. John 8:7 (KJV).
x. John 8:9 (KJV).
xi. John 8:9 (KJV).
xii. John 8:44 (KJV).

5. LET'S THINK WITH OUR HEADS

i. 1 Timothy 3:12.

6. HOW WHITE ANXIETY THRIVES

i. Mark 12:30–31 (KJV).
ii. Luke 10:29 (KJV).
iii. Luke 10:36–37 (KJV).
iv. Mark 12:30–31 (KJV).

7. CONSERVATIVES AND WHITE ANXIETY'S HISTORY

i. census.gov
ii. George C. Rable, But There Was No Peace: The Role of Violence in the Politics of Reconstruction (University of Georgia Press, 1984).
iii. Keni Hines, A Global History of Blacks in the 19th Century: Detailed Chronologically from 1800 to 1899 (Armstrong Smith, 2021).
iv. Kyle Whitmire, "Ambushed in Eufaula: Alabama's Forgotten Race Massacre," AL.com, last updated March 14, 2023, https://www.al.com/news/2022/01/ambushed-in-eufaula-alabamas-forgotten-race-massacre.html.
v. Williams v. Mississippi, 170 U.S. 213 (1898)
vi. Barry Goldwater, *The Conscience of a Conservative* (Victor Publishing, 1960)
vii. Brown v. Board of Education of Topeka, 347 U.S. 483 (1954)
viii. Keni Hines, *A Global History of Blacks in the 19th Century: Detailed Chronologically from 1800 to 1899* (Armstrong Smith, 2021).
ix. Luke A. Nichter, The Year That Broke Politics: Collusion and Chaos in the Presidential Election of 1968 (Yale University Press, 2023).
x. Cohen, Richard M.; Witcover, Jules (1974). A Heartbeat Away: The Investigation and Resignation of Vice President Spiro T. Agnew. New York: The Viking Press.
xi. Seth Cagin and Philip Dray, We Are Not Afraid: The Story of Goodman, Schwerner, and Chaney (Nation Books, 2006).

8. REPUBLICANS AND BAD ECONOMIES

i. Julie Zauzmer et al., "'Wasted Our Lives': Catholic Sex Abuse Scandals Again Prompt a Crisis of Faith," *Washington Post*, August 19, 2018, https://www.washingtonpost.com/news/acts-of-faith/wp/2018/08/19/wasted-our-lives-catholic-sex-abuse-scandals-again-prompt-a-crisis-of-faith/.

ii. April 10, 1980, Carnegie Melon University speech.
iii. [Citation for the Reagan content—the original citation here related to the Bush content]

9. POOR PERFORMANCE AND BAD BEHAVIOR

i. Psalm 116:11 (KJV).

10. CONSERVATIVES MUST COME CLEAN

i. Debra Cassens Weiss, "Scalia on Bush v. Gore: 'Get Over It,'" *ABA Journal*, March 10, 2008, https://www.abajournal.com/news/article/scalia_on_bush_v_gore_get_over_it.

11. WEALTH CONCENTRATION HURTS US ALL

i. Citizens United v. Federal Election Commission, 558 U.S. 310 (2010).

12. DEMOCRATS MUST MESSAGE

i. Commission on Presidential Debates, 2012 Vice Presidential Debate, October 11, 2012.

13. STEPS TOWARD BETTER CHOICES

i. Henry Hazlitt, *Economics in One Lesson* (Harper & Brothers, 1948).

14. CONCLUSION

i. California Governor Ronald Reagan, Inaugural Address, January 6, 1967
ii. Irving Dilliard, ed., Mr. Justice Brandeis: Great American (Modern View Press, 1941), 42.

INDEX

A

Abortion, 48, 90
Affordable Care Act (ACA), 40
Afghanistan War, 154
Agnew, Spiro, 117, 141
A-Mark Foundation, 27, 146
Angelou, Maya, xvii
Automakers (Big Three), bankruptcy and bailout of, 13, 17–18, 122, 153
Automation, and job loss, 162

B

Balanced Budget Act, 50–51, 133
Bankruptcy, corporate and personal, 13, 84, 122, 152, 153
Bible, cited in argument, xii, 10, 26, 45, 48, 53, 73, 90, 104, 105
Biden, Joe, 16, 17, 61, 62, 83, 124, 133, 144, 145, 161, 170, 171, 173–175
Bloody Sunday (1965), 51, 116
Brandeis, Louis (Justice), 15–16, 190
Brown v. Board of Education, 113
Buffett, Warren, 1
Build Back Better Act (2021), 161
Bureau of Labor Statistics (BLS), 131
Bush, George H. W., xii, xiii, 3, 13, 94, 120, 137, 140, 142
Bush, George W., 5, 8, 12, 13, 28, 37, 51, 93, 94, 121, 131, 142, 151, 174

C

Cabinet, presidential, 168
Capitalism, 49
Carried interest (tax loophole), 161
Carroll, E. Jean, 39
Carter, Jimmy, xi, 15, 26, 93, 118, 121, 129
Catholic Church, 134–135
China, trade with, 17–18
Church, role of, xii, 26, 71, 81, 90–92, 134, 135
Citizens United v. FEC, 160
Civil Rights Act of 1964, 47, 99, 103, 113, 115, 118
Civil Rights Movement, 52, 99, 113–115
 see also Montgomery bus boycott; Selma; Voting Rights Act
Civil War, xviii, 29, 32–33, 36, 46, 67–68, 100, 110
 see also Confederate States of America; secession; slavery
Class system, American, xvii–xviii
Clinton, Bill, 3, 13, 28, 50, 132, 133, 138, 149, 151–153, 170, 181, 185
Clinton, Hillary, 95, 124, 153, 161
Confederate States of America (CSA), xxi, 33, 35, 36, 111–113, 116, 125, 141
Congresses, Republican vs. Democratic, fiscal claims about, 129, 136
Constitution, U.S., 31–32, 35
 Article I, 32, 96, 114, 145, 189
 Article V, 38, 52, 54
 Article VI, 52
 Tenth Amendment, 100, 114
 Thirteenth Amendment, 46, 55
 Fourteenth Amendment, 67
 Fifteenth Amendment, 47, 52, 109–110, 112, 114
Constitutional Convention, 30–31, 33
Continental Congress, 30
Coolidge, Calvin, 28, 133, 170
Corporate tax, 95
COVID-19 pandemic, 123, 131

D

Davis, Jefferson, 33, 35–37, 50
Debates, presidential, 62, 89, 172, 173, 175

Deficit, federal, xiv, xx, 8–10, 12–13, 15, 17, 19, 27–28, 50–51, 55, 70, 94–95, 121–125, 132–133, 135–138, 146, 149, 151–154, 158, 168–170, 175, 181, 184–185
  under Reagan, 137–138
  under G. W. Bush, 94, 121
  under Trump, 136–138, 146
Democratic National Convention (1936), 86
Democratic Party, xxi, 8, 13, 15–16, 56, 59, 86, 100, 113, 115–116, 118
  messaging strategy for, 167–178
Detroit, x–xii, 11, 77–78, 131, 138, 151, 153, 163
Dodd-Frank Act (2010), 161
Dog-whistle politics, 118

E

Eisenhower, Dwight D., 5, 7, 8, 68
Election Day, xix, 14–18, 63, 109–111, 113, 116, 171
Emancipation Proclamation, 46
Emotion versus reason, xxii, 12–14, 17, 19–20, 41, 43, 59–60, 66–67, 74–75, 77, 79–80, 85, 87–88, 90–92, 95–96, 100–101, 107, 115, 138–139, 141, 147, 187, 190
Executive orders, 46

F

Farmers and farm economy, 17–18, 78–79, 103, 125, 130, 168, 171
Fear, as political strategy, xv, xix, xxii, 8, 33–35, 42, 57–61, 63–64, 67, 68, 71, 75, 80–81, 88, 96, 134
Federal deficit, *see Deficit, federal*
Ford, Gerald, 117–118
Foreclosure crisis, xiii, 153
Founding Fathers, 134
Framers of the Constitution, 38, 45, 53
Freedom Summer (1964), 120

G

GDP (gross domestic product) and growth, 2, 19, 125, 140, 157, 167, 172, 180
Goldwater, Barry, 99–100, 113, 118
Good Samaritan, parable of, 105–107
Grant, Ulysses S., 110, 114, 125
Great Depression, xiii–xiv, 5, 8, 10, 16–17, 20, 27, 29, 51, 62, 68–69, 85, 94, 131, 133, 151, 153, 154, 157–158, 164–165, 170
Great Migration, x
Great Recession (2008), 5, 12, 94, 121–122, 131, 151–152
Grooming, of voters, xvii, xxii, 58–64, 183–184

H

Harding, Warren G., 13
Harris, Kamala, 83, 136
Healthcare policy, 40–41, 103, 140, 148
Homelessness, 53, 158
Hoover, Herbert, xiii, 7–8, 20, 51, 62, 68, 85, 164
House of Representatives, 31, 35, 40, 50, 135, 141, 143
Humphrey, Hubert, 99, 116

I

Immigration, 90, 123
Impeachment, 141, 143–145
Income tax, 138, 159–161
Inflation, 125, 129–131, 161
Inflation Reduction Act (2022), 161
Infrastructure spending, 158
Inheritance and estate planning, 190
Integration, school, 114
Iraq War, 142–143, 154
IRS Code, 160

J

January 6 (2021), 146
Johnson, Lyndon B., 7, 52, 99, 113, 116, 118–119, 124

Jobs, creation and growth of, 132, 167, 171

K

Kennedy, John F., 7, 52, 66, 113
Keynes, John Maynard, 5
King, Martin Luther, Jr., xv
Ku Klux Klan, xviii, 67

L

Labor unions, 29, 33, 48, 162, 163
Layoffs, 166
Limbaugh, Rush, xi, 140, 184
Lincoln, Abraham, 34–36, 41, 46, 110, 115
Logic versus emotion, *see Emotion versus reason*
Lynching, 102

M

Manufacturing, decline and offshoring of, 163–164
McConnell, Mitch, 145
Media, role of, xii, 35, 39, 59, 64, 84, 88, 94, 125, 140, 149–152, 182–184
Medicaid, 37
Medicare, 37, 88
Meritocracy, xxii
Middle class, 70, 173
Mississippi Plan (1890), 100, 111, 112
Montgomery bus boycott, 52, 116

N

National Bureau of Economic Research (NBER), 4–5, 152
National debt, xii–xiii, xx, 16, 28, 94, 133, 136–137, 157–158, 162, 174, 176
New Deal, 7
New Testament, cited, 104–105
Nixon, Richard, xi, 7, 25, 29, 70, 116–118, 131, 141, 175
Norquist, Grover, 23, 37, 42, 56
North Carolina, x, 112, 120, 122, 130

O

Obama, Barack, 13, 40, 94, 122–124, 133, 152, 153, 161, 170
Oil and gas prices, xi, xiv, 106, 125
Omnibus Budget Reconciliation Act, 50, 133

P

Party politics, need for two productive parties, 1–21
Payroll tax (FICA), 166
Poverty, 147, 148
Productivity, worker, 159

R

Race, and political identity
  Black Americans, 68, 101
  Black Liberals, 45, 55, 110, 112
  White Americans, xix, 71, 101
  White Conservatives, 58–59, 67, 100–101, 110–113, 115
Racism, 62, 86, 88
Reagan, Ronald, xi–xiii, 3, 5, 16, 26–27, 29, 37, 42, 50, 87, 119–120, 129–131, 133, 137–138, 140, 142, 150, 157, 162, 165, 173–174, 176, 180–181, 183, 190
  economic record of, 129–131, 137–138, 150
  tax policy of, 3, 137
  deregulation under, 129–130
Reaganomics, 137
Recession, xi–xv, xx, 3–13, 15–17, 19, 42, 62, 64, 70, 94, 95, 120–122, 129–132, 138, 140, 148–150, 152, 154, 168, 176, 181, 184
Religion, xx
  see also Bible, cited in argument; Church, role of
Republican Party, xviii, xxi, 2–3, 8, 14–15, 17, 20, 25–26, 29, 39, 42, 47, 60, 68, 87, 99–100, 111, 115, 118–119, 126, 135, 155, 175
Romney, Mitt, 145, 173

Roosevelt, Franklin D., 7, 20, 85, 122, 158, 164
Running mate, selection of, 173
Ryan, Paul, 173–175

S

Secession, 33
Segregation, xviii, 99, 113, 118
Selma, Alabama, 52, 116
Senate, U.S., 12, 20, 31, 35, 40, 50, 52, 54, 89, 94, 116, 135, 141–145, 175
Sharecropping, 130
Slavery, xviii, 33–36, 46–47, 54–55, 67, 125
Snake oil, as political metaphor, xiv
Social Security, 85–87, 158
South Carolina, 34, 109, 111, 112, 114, 120
Southern strategy, 119, 138
Stock market, and crashes, 20, 64, 164
Strikes, labor, 162
Supply-side economics, 3, 13–17, 19–20, 42, 85, 95, 129, 136–137, 154, 180, 190
Supreme Court, xviii, 15, 30–31, 47, 113, 135, 151, 160

T

Talk radio, xi
Tariffs, 18, 103, 164
Tax cuts, 3, 15, 20, 37, 62–63, 94, 123, 137, 151, 154, 161–162, 173–175, 180–181
Tax Cuts and Jobs Act (2017), 161
Tennessee Valley Authority, 51, 69
Terrorism, xviii, 67, 100
Trickle-down economics, *see Supply-side economics*
Trump, Donald, xix, xx, 16–18, 25, 26, 28, 37, 39, 40, 61, 62, 65, 83, 86, 93–95, 123–125, 131, 133, 136, 137, 141, 143–146, 161, 168, 169, 171
  economic record of, 16–18, 123–125, 131, 136–138
  impeachments of, 141, 143–145
  2024 campaign of, 61–62, 65, 83

U

Unemployment, xiv, xx, 2, 6–13, 16, 19, 68–69, 85, 94–95, 103, 120–125, 131–132, 140, 153–154, 164, 170–171
United States Constitution, *see Constitution, U.S.*
USMCA (trade agreement), 18

V

Vice presidency, 3, 13, 117, 137, 141, 142, 175
Vicksburg Massacre (1874), 110–111, 114
Voter registration, 99, 112
Voter suppression, 113–114
Voting Rights Act of 1965, 47, 52, 113–116, 118

W

Wages, 72, 163
Wallace, George, 116–118
Watergate, 7, 117–118, 141
Wealth concentration, 16, 157, 159, 161–163, 165, 190
  chapter-length treatment of, 157–166
White Anxiety (concept), throughout
  definition of, 57–76
  history of, in Conservative politics, 109–128
  how it thrives, 99–108
White House, 28, 46, 141, 186
World War II, 69

ABOUT THE AUTHOR

Douglas Hines has a talent for spotting the trends in statistics. Doug owns a company that developed baseball scoring systems used by Major League Baseball teams and broadcasters to calculate and display player, team, and game information during their games. His systems have populated scoreboards in stadiums all over the country for decades.

With a background in computer science and mathematics, Doug takes a deep dive into economic data and explains the important role the economy and racialized fear play in the choices we make during elections.

For his entire career, Doug has related very complex concepts and statistics to the public in ways that they could easily consume. His writing relates his more than fifty years of experience with America's economy as a citizen in our political and economic environment.

Douglas has been married since 1983 and is the father of six children and eleven grandchildren. Doug and his wife work together in their software business.

Douglas also serves as a deacon in his local congregation of the Church of Christ.

www.ingramcontent.com/pod-product-compliance
Lightning Source LLC
LaVergne TN
LVHW042057230926
848801LV00007B/156

* 9 7 9 8 9 9 4 9 4 1 5 2 2 *